INSANE ROOTS

INSANE ROOTS
The Adventures of a Con-Artist and Her Daughter

A MEMOIR

forward by KERRY FINA

Tiffany Rochelle

New York

INSANE ROOTS
The Adventures of a Con-Artist and Her Daughter

A MEMOIR

© 2016 Tiffany Rochelle.

Published in New York, New York, by Morgan James Publishing. Morgan James and The Entrepreneurial Publisher are trademarks of Morgan James, LLC.
www.MorganJamesPublishing.com

The Morgan James Speakers Group can bring authors to your live event. For more information or to book an event visit The Morgan James Speakers Group at www.TheMorganJamesSpeakersGroup.com.

Disclaimer: The experiences in this memoir are depicted based on the author's memory and the story telling of others. While all the events in this book are true, some names and identifying characteristics have been changed to protect the privacy of the people involved.

A **free** eBook edition is available with the purchase of this print book.

CLEARLY PRINT YOUR NAME ABOVE IN UPPER CASE

Instructions to claim your free eBook edition:
1. Download the BitLit app for Android or iOS
2. Write your name in **UPPER CASE** on the line
3. Use the BitLit app to submit a photo
4. Download your eBook to any device

ISBN 978-1-63047-629-8 paperback
ISBN 978-1-63047-630-4 eBook
Library of Congress Control Number:
2015906391

Cover Design by:
Rachel Lopez
www.r2cdesign.com

Interior Design by:
Bonnie Bushman
The Whole Caboodle Graphic Design

In an effort to support local communities and raise awareness and funds, Morgan James Publishing donates a percentage of all book sales for the life of each book to Habitat for Humanity Peninsula and Greater Williamsburg

Get involved today, visit
www.MorganJamesBuilds.com

Habitat for Humanity®
Peninsula and
Greater Williamsburg
Building Partner

To Karen,
Your time with us was ever so short,
but the impact you have had on
many of our lives will last forever.

Table of Contents

Foreword   *ix*

Acknowledgments   *xi*

Chapter One   **1**

My Crazy Mother . . .   2

How Did I Get Here?   6

According to My Mother . . .   9

Building a Life   13

My Mother and I Disappeared   16

One Year Later, We Reappeared   19

Starting Over Again   22

Chapter Two   **29**

My First Stepfather   30

And So the Travels Begin . . .   34

Surprise!   41

South Dakota   43

Chapter 3   **47**
    The Accident   48
    My New Home   54
    Christmas   57
    Wait . . . What?   59

Chapter 4   **63**
    The Identity Crisis   64
    Feeling at Home   68
    Living with a Cast   71

Chapter 5   **75**
    Ready, Set, Sled!   76
    Easter   79
    Summer Fun   84
    Vacation!   87
    Change of Plans   89

Chapter 6   **93**
    My New Life   94
    The Ice Cream Shop   97
    Our New Home   100
    My Mother's New Girlfriend   102
    Let's Go!   108

Chapter 7 **113**

    Florida 114

    The Flight 117

    Time Served 119

Chapter 8 **121**

    Moving On 122

    My Best Friend 129

    Halloween 1995 132

    Our New Puppy! 134

    Unwrapped 136

    D.C. Trip 139

Chapter 9 **143**

    Mother's New Friends 144

    What's Up with Mom? 148

    Again? 151

    She Is Alive 154

    Mixed Feelings 156

    Afterword 161

Foreword

By Kerry Fina

I didn't sleep that night. I watched her, and I listened to her breathe. Sporadically, she would wake up afraid, but it only took a moment to comfort her each time. There had been a lot of sleepless nights lately, wondering where she was, if she was okay, if I would ever see her again. Now, she was here, but her little eight-year-old body had taken a beating. She was a tough kid—she'd never had a choice in that matter. Whatever physical harm she had endured could not diminish the inner warrior on whom she had relied for emotional and psychological protection since the day she was born.

I only had a few hours to spend with her now. She had come into my life just two years earlier, but my heart was breaking as if we'd been father and daughter her whole life. Everything would change. I knew I wouldn't see her for a very long time. I might never see her again. Ironically, the journey that had literally started with "Joy" quickly became a nightmare that would leave many people hurt and scarred. At the time, I feared mostly for the kid—it would be extraordinary for her to grow up sane and live a normal, happy life. Despite the strange circumstances of her childhood as the daughter of a sociopath, she did maintain stability. She did live happily, and she took it one step further: She somehow found a way to bring more happiness into the world.

In her deftly written memoir, Tiffany gives us a very personal look into her childhood, through her eyes. It is, at times, horrifying, bizarre, and humorous. But, around every hard edge there is love—love from within, love from a stranger, and love from an extended but fiercely loyal family.

Byron wrote, " 'Tis strange — but true; for truth is always strange; Stranger than fiction; . . ." Keep that in mind as you look through this window into Tiffany's life.

Acknowledgments

To all of those who were present in my early life and those still very much a part of my life today: Although your characters may be missing from the pages of this book, please know that it does not mean you are forgotten. The love and kindness you have all shown to me will forever fill my heart.

To my editor, Angela Pica, thank you for seeing my vision and putting into words what I find myself struggling to express. I value your opinion and appreciate all that you are.

To my godfamily, thank you for accepting me into your family, supporting me, and loving me unconditionally. This book would not have been possible without the support and encouragement of my dearest friends. Thank you for believing in me.

Words cannot express my gratitude to my stepfather, Kerry Fina. His clarity of the many milestones in my youth have made it possible for me to piece this story together.

To my mother, my insane roots, if it was not for you, I would have no story. Thank you for the many misadventures and, most important, the gift of life.

Chapter One

My Crazy Mother . . .

They say a mother's love is the most generous love of all. But what if the love she has for herself is so much more important that she forgets about everyone else? Is it possible that her actions may merely be the result of her regrets from a life she never had a chance to live? The only living result of which she can claim no credit for: her daughter. Strong, resilient, and determined. All qualities that may not have been taught to her by her mother, but surely hold themselves as the result of her actions. A lifetime filled with pain, deceit, and unanswered questions.

Trying to find oneself amongst a past that is scarcely dim with truth, yet sturdily iridescent with hope, oh where to begin! I do have fond memories of our time together, yet every time they begin to take me away I end up bumping into the grief of their vagrant existence. A little girl so filled with hope that her eyes sparkle, only to be let down by the one person she needed to lift her up. I have always felt somewhat less like a daughter and more like a convenient addition to my mother's con-schemes; no one would suspect a mother and her sweet little girl.

Looking back, I revel in the amazement of how oblivious one can be to the ridiculous behavior that is so obviously displayed in front of them. It is amazing what one can choose not to notice or find a way to justify from the need for normalcy. Sometimes the painful truth is just too much for a child to handle.

Like the time my mother and I went car shopping. At the time my mother drove an old VW beetle. I loved that car! It was dark green with matching leather interior and roll-down windows. There was a large gap between the window glass and its frame where I would slide papers and things when I was waiting for my mom. Which is exactly what I was doing on this particular occasion while my mother spoke with a nice-looking salesman in the parking lot of a dealership near our home. As I watched them through the window, I began to sense that something was about to happen. The man escorted my mother from vehicle to vehicle as she opened the doors and sat in each one. Before long, the salesman left my mother and walked inside the showroom of the dealership. As he faded out of site, my mother motioned me to roll down the window in the car and told me to gather my things.

"We are taking a test ride in a new vehicle!" she exclaimed.

"Can I leave my book?" I asked.

"No, you need to take everything," she replied sternly.

Before I could say anything else, the salesman was back and handing my mother a key to a small black car he had just pulled up in next to us.

As the salesman waved us out of the lot, I tapped on my mother's shoulder from the backseat and asked, "Mom . . . are we stealing this car?"

Looking at me through the rearview mirror, she replied in a very calm voice, "No honey. We are borrowing it," and then she looked away.

I knew in my heart that wasn't true, but I chose not to ask any more questions.

The more I begin to write, the more I begin to remember. The hardest part of trying to start my story is coming to grips with the reality of its truth. Putting it into words somehow makes it more real than it ever was while I was living it. At the time I was experiencing it, I was focused on getting through it. Now that I am reflecting on it, I am having to really understand the gravity of it all.

In the best description, I spent my early childhood as a fly on the wall of my mother's crazy life. Have you ever talked to a fly? I bet it would have a lot of interesting things to say! I know I do. . . .

My mother is so many different people, and if anyone knows the real lady underneath all the baggage, it would be me. Keep in mind, however, that this is a women who barely knows herself and therefore the "real" deal is sometimes hard to find. Although my time with her has been limited, I would never change a thing. I am who I am as a result of her actions. I like to think there is a little good in everyone, and I hope this book can give insight and understanding to those whose lives she touched in some way—good or bad. I have been blessed with so many wonderful people in my life that I would never risk losing just one of them for the changing of a moment. She made life so much more interesting than it would have been if I'd had an "ordinary" childhood. We had extraordinary adventures and met a million friends along the way!

If my mother had been more straight edge and wholesome, I may have missed meeting the people I now hold dearest to me. My life might have been less chaotic, but I am not sure I would be the person I am had it been any different. Please enjoy the tale of our excursions and remember the phrase, "You can't choose your family." It has so much relevance.

How Did I Get Here?

T he conception of me is a bit fuzzy, but rumor has it that my mother met a lovely man in a pub near or in Corning, New York. According to the hospital records, my father was one of the men she was seeing at the time. He denies any connection to me and, knowing her, I don't blame him.

Regardless of when or with whom, nine months later, there I was!

Most people in her situation may have thought of a baby as just another burden, but to her I was nothing short of a jackpot. After all, saying no to a strung-out teen was easy, but a mother hard on her luck . . . Never!

As are the details of my conception, so are the details of my birth. The story my mother told me was much more interesting than the real one, I am sure, and this one includes my real dad, so I like it, even if I know it isn't true. I believed it for years and it gave tragic personality and love to the rumor of a one-night stand.

My mother, in her early twenties, dated a terribly troubled alcoholic. Whom she met in New York after fleeing her abusive parents in Texas. She rarely spoke of him and I am not able to remember a single time she described him physically to me. I remember her telling me of his native heritage and kind eyes, but nothing descriptive. Looking back, I really should have asked. I wish I would have asked.

They had only been "dating" for a few months when she told him she was pregnant. Apparently, he had been drinking and didn't take the news well. They argued and the fight ended with him pushing her down the stairs of their apartment building. She left him and drove to Pennsylvania, where she stayed in sporadic communication with him and claims he was trying to get sober.

A few months later, she went into labor with me. Before she went to the hospital she called my father and he told her he was on his way. Unfortunately he had been drinking and, I need not elaborate, he never made it.

Knowing now that she manufactured this elaborate tragedy to explain my birth rather than face the hopeless reality of her situation (and mine) gives me some insight into my mother's mind. What an utterly sad place she must have been in to need to create the fake existence she used to live the rest of her life.

According to My Mother . . .

T his is the point in the story where I usually get so frustrated in attempting to arrange the scattered memories and stories within the factual timeline of my early childhood that I stop writing. I told myself that I was not going to give up so easily this time. I was bound and determined to organize the details of our life together. I knew it was a necessary process for me to grow as a person, by working through some of the harsh memories that I have cut out of my mind. A part of me was afraid to take this step into the past, but I knew I was ready to face whatever I would find.

The early years were a time in my life when my mother's presence was the most consistent. And since for the first few years of my life I have no memory of any of the events that occurred, I am forced to rely on her for nearly all explanation. Considering the dramatic rendition of my birth, one can only assume that many of the other stories told to me may also contain some slight exaggerations. That is not to say that her account of these years was not somewhat accurate and inspired by, if not fully rooted in, the truth.

That having been said, according to my mother, she was living in her car in Pennsylvania when she went into labor. She had been working for an assisted living group as a caretaker and planned to rent an apartment as soon as she had enough money saved.

She spent her time in the recovery room watching soap operas and waiting for my father to arrive. This soap opera ended up being the source for my first name, although I've never checked to see if that was even possible. Sometime throughout her stay in the hospital, she met with the chaplain on staff. She told him her story and he offered to help. This one chance meeting opened up a whole new beginning for her.

It turns out that he was the pastor at a nearby church, which had a network of parishioners who offered help to those who needed it. These good-hearted people assisted in finding her and her newborn baby a home. There were so many people who took us in and helped us out during the first years of my life.

She told everyone the poetic story of my father's race to the hospital that ended in tragedy, and further explained that she had no savings and no place to live. The story being so heartbreaking, she was never questioned. Instead, she was showered with resources! For two years we bounced around from family to family, from kind soul to kind soul.

I cannot express enough how crucial these early relationships were in forming the person I am today. Regardless of how their contact with my mother ended, their love and support for me never did. I am beyond thankful for every single one of them.

From the facts that I have pieced together, I know confidently that the majority of her account is true and accurate.

The entire story about my father, on the other hand, is absolutely false. He was not killed in a car accident on the way to witness the birth of his baby girl. In fact, I am pretty sure he had no idea that any of it was even happening. My mother never told me the truth about any of it, except for the part about them meeting in a pub in or around Corning, New York. That part could be true.

I made contact with my real father once. Well, if you call being on the other end of a three-way call contact. I can't remember exactly how old I was, but I know I was at my godparents' house (either living there or visiting). My best friend from our church found his phone number by searching for the name listed on my birth certificate in the Corning, New York, area. She called him while I listened in. After she confirmed that she was talking to a man by the correct name, she asked him if he knew my mother. He told her yes, but you could hear the reluctance in his voice to answer any further questions. My friend explained to him that she was calling on my behalf and that I was not looking for anything; I just wanted to know if he was indeed my father. He told her he was "real sorry" but that my mother was running around with a whole slew of men so he could not be sure if I was actually his.

That is all I remember of the conversation. I never tried contacting him again.

Building a Life

Perhaps the most significant moment of my young life, although I was oblivious to it at the time, was when my mother and I moved in with the people who later became my godparents. We met them through the church just as we had met many other caring families who took us in. The bond I formed with them, however, was like none other. In present day, I refer to them as my mother and father and their children as my brother and sister, but that story comes later.

Eventually, they helped her to make arrangements to buy a VW beetle and rent an apartment. This, I am told, was where we had my second birthday party. We were buying the rugged old bug from the same lady who rented us the basement in her house. This was the first time we lived in a place where we had to pay rent. Prior to this, my mother just pitched in around the house to help whichever family we were staying with to earn our keep. The apartment was just big enough for the two of us. We had our own private entrance in the back of the house. Our front door opened into a nice-size kitchen that sat next to the living room. There was a bedroom that we shared. Mostly it was just there to house all of our stuff. Whenever my mother wasn't dating someone, we usually slept together on the couch.

Mom did start dating again after we were settled. Though I don't remember much about that man, except for what she has told me over the years, and most of it was not good. The majority of her stories about him involved his raging temper and consumption of large amounts of alcohol. It was with the two of them that I had my first taste of wine, and the first time I actually got drunk. I am not sure who had the idea, but one of them decided to give me some wine to calm me down because I was being too hyper. I was only a few years old and apparently had too much energy for them. Unfortunately, it did not calm me down. It pumped me up. My mother began to worry and decided to take me to my godparents' house for help.

By the time our dusty old beetle pulled into the familiar driveway, my eyes were bloodshot and I was beginning to sweat. She barely finished slowing down before her door flew open and she ran to my side of the car. Quickly, she pulled my sweaty body from the backseat. I tried to walk by myself, but she gave up on my lack of motor skills, scooped me up, and walked down the cement path. She knocked with panicked repetition on the door until my godmother answered. Her eyes locked with mine immediately. In a very stern voice she asked, "What is going on?"

My mother mumbled, "Is it okay to give a child alcohol?"

My godmother paused and then, with a mild roar, she exclaimed, "Heavens no! Are you kidding? What were you thinking? How much did you give her? What did you give her?"

Defending herself, my mother yelled, "She was running around like crazy and we just thought a few sips would calm her down. Mothers give it to their babies when they are teething!"

"Yeah, a drop on the finger to cut the pain, not enough to make them drunk!" my godmother rebuked as she grabbed me from my mother's arms.

She didn't bother to inquire anymore; it was clear I had obviously had too much. My eyes were glazed over, my body was sweaty, and I couldn't make much sense of anything. She spent the rest of the night walking me around to keep me awake and coaxing me to drink as much water as possible.

The effects of the alcohol eventually wore off and things calmed down. Little did I know that chaotic events such as these would become something I would grow to consider normal for many years to come.

My Mother and I Disappeared

n April of 1985, when I was two and a half years old, my mother and I disappeared. The boyfriend I have mentioned previously found out that she had been stealing from him. As a result, she was charged with theft. Before she could be arrested, we were gone. When we left, we used our trusty old beetle as our getaway car. Unfortunately, my godfather had cosigned the agreement to purchase this beetle from our landlord, Bettie. He had done the same on the lease agreement for the apartment we rented. When Mom skipped out on the rent and the car, Bettie filed charges against my mother for theft. And since we were nowhere to be found, who was left to pick up the pieces? That's right: my godfather. Bettie sued him for the cost of the car and the rent for the apartment.

They were able to come to an agreement where he would pay the money owed and Bettie would drop the grand theft charge on my mother. However, she would still be charged with forgery for the worthless checks she had written to Bettie for the rent. Once that was settled, my godparents decided to hire a private detective to find us: Detective Honey. Knowing the little bit they did about my mother, they thought this type of behavior was out of the ordinary and completely irrational.

I found out years later that my mother actually had taken off to Illinois to visit her family. The family that for several years prior had had no idea where she was. Unlike my godparents, they were used to her random disappearances and reappearances. The only difference this time was that she wasn't alone.

Meanwhile, my godparents worried and the search for us continued. A few months passed before they received a call from the detective. He was sure he had located my mother and asked that they come into his office to identify a photo. The person the detective had located was a woman from Pampa, Texas, with the same name and birth date as my mother. There was no sign of me, but he was positive it was her. There was no sign of the car, but he figured she would have ditched it as soon as she could since it was now technically stolen.

Feeling they had finally made some progress, my godparents walked into Detective Honey's office with confidence. With pride, the detective held up the photo of the women he had found and waited to hear them rejoice. But to his surprise, they did not celebrate. The woman in the photo looked nothing like my mother; not even close. They had not made any progress after all. If anything, this only raised more questions.

One Year Later, We Reappeared

n April of 1986, my mother and I flew back to Pennsylvania. After having been gone for almost a year, and having had no contact with anyone. My mother called my godmother from the airport to ask for a ride. She agreed to pick us up if my mother agreed to turn herself in the next morning. She complied and I was able to stay with my godparents while she served her time. She was then released on probation. I was too young to understand any of this. All I knew was that I was able to stay with my godparents, and I loved it!

After a few months, my godmother convinced my mother to start Christian counseling and offered to pay for her sessions. It was with a woman counselor who operated out of her home and had a daughter right around my age. In the beginning, the three of us would go together. I would hang out in the waiting room with the counselor's daughter and we would pretend to read my godmother stories while we waited. Once my godmother was sure my mother was on track with her counseling, she stopped staying for her sessions and spent the time running errands instead. My mother's counseling routine only lasted a little while, until she was convinced she was "better" and eventually she started keeping the money for her sessions instead of actually going. When my godparents finally found out, they had no choice but to ask her to leave their home. She had been living there for about a year and for several months she had been slowly stealing from them. Items had gone missing, in addition to the money she had been keeping from her counseling sessions, and they simply were no longer able to trust her.

Unsure where to go, my mother drove to the home of my godmother's best friend, Karen. Another person who will forever hold a very special place in my heart. She told me this story when I was in my early twenties in one of the last meaningful moments I shared with her. It was told to me as an example of the importance of faith.

Karen was sitting in the kitchen when something made her stand up. Through the living room window, directly across from her, she was able to see my mother's car coming down the driveway. What she saw on her walk to the door appalled her. Karen watched as my mother bent down to tell me something and then pinched my upper arm until I cried. She then grabbed my hand and began walking toward the door. Now standing behind the door, Karen waited for the knock. Composing herself and trying to appear oblivious, she answered. My mother told her I was crying because my godparents had kicked us out and we had no place to live. She asked if we would be able to live with her until we were back on our feet. Karen paused in reflection.

Had she not been privy to my mother's previous actions, she would have taken us in with no question. Making herself vulnerable to the same misdoings to which many others had fallen victim. Allowing us to stay could have devastated her.

So, as hard as it was, her answer to my mother was a very firm no. She said it broke her heart to see me cry and she wanted more than anything to scoop me up and take me away, but she knew it was just not possible. Instead, she closed the door and prayed. A prayer she continued for many years after.

Starting Over Again

——————————

After we moved out of my godparents' house, my mother used the same story she had tried with Karen to lure someone else into taking us in. We never stayed in one place too long. My mother used to tell me it was not polite to overstay your welcome anywhere, but I am not sure that is the real reason we moved around. Regardless, I thought it was pretty cool. Everyone we stayed with was different in their own way and I enjoyed experiencing the wide varieties of family life.

We stayed with one family where music was alive in every room. Everyone had a musical talent of some sort, and after dinner each night everyone would show them off during a family sing-along! It was great!

Another family we stayed with had an older daughter who I admired so much. I thought she was just the coolest! She used to babysit me while my mother worked. Unfortunately during this time, she acquired chicken pox from me, for which I thought I would never be forgiven. She did forgive me and started calling me her little chicken pox for years to follow.

At one point, my mother moved in with a very dear friend of hers. I called her Emma. She was the equivalent of a grandmother to me; overly kind, warm, and always ready to spoil me!

Emma lived with her husband, just minutes from my godparents and our church. Their house was set back in the woods at the top of a very steep hill. In heavy snowfalls our car would always get stuck trying to make it up the hill. We would get about halfway to the top and it just wouldn't go any farther. My mother would usually get out and try to push, but it never helped. We ended up walking the rest of the way every time.

Emma had a variety of cats, dogs, and chickens running around outside. There was one dog they kept chained up behind the chicken coop who I was told never to go near. He was a rescue dog and he was not very friendly. He would go to Emma's husband, but no one else dared to go near him. That scared me a little.

Emma also had a cockatiel she kept in a cage in the kitchen who would never be quiet. I remember them arguing back and forth constantly. As the bickering escalated, she would get so frustrated that she would threaten to put him in the oven.

He would squawk "pretty bird, pretty bird" over and over again.

Until finally Emma would yell, "If you don't can it, I'll bake you for supper!"

To which he would reply, "Ooooohhhh, pretty bird, pretty bird!"

It would go on and on like that, until eventually, Emma would throw something in his direction or she would just give up. He never made it to the oven, but there were times it came really close!

I thought it was hilarious!

Emma had several sons, but the one my mother dated was always my favorite. He was the definition of fantastic as far as I was concerned. Howdy was a very muscular man with broad shoulders and a multitude of tattoos. His voice was deep and strong. A voice one hears and immediately stops to listen to. I remember hearing my mother and Emma talk about his bad temper, but he was always wonderfully nice to me. Not to mention, he had a habit for bringing me stuffed animals that were as large if not larger than I was. First it was a gray dog standing as tall as me that doubled as a puppet. There was a hole in the back of his head that you could put your hand in to make him talk. Then, a few months later he brought me a bear that was equally as large and dressed in a plaid shirt and overalls.

I am not sure why my mother and Howdy parted ways, but I do know how they did. One day he came over to our new apartment and she greeted him with a wall. She refused his gifts and told him to leave. Just like that, it was over. I have asked her many times to elaborate, but she would never tell me. Over time, they reconnected and stayed friends. As did my mother and Emma for many years to come. I was so young and I am sure there was a lot that I missed. To be honest, that is perfectly fine. I have seen the negative side of numerous people, so it's refreshing to hold someone under a solely positive ray.

Although I don't remember it vividly, in September of 1987 I started school! It was just after my fifth birthday; I barely made the cutoff. It was the first time ever that I had attended school. Photos of me prior to this time are virtually nonexistent, so I am very lucky to have a picture of myself standing on the front steps of school on my first day of kindergarten. All I remember is being extremely excited! Every day, on the way to school, my mother and I would stop and get chocolate doughnuts and chocolate milk for breakfast. After school I would go with Mom to the nursing home where she worked. When she was busy, I visited with the numerous residents and "smoked" candy cigarettes with everyone in the smokers' lounge. I loved it!

It wasn't very long before I was graduating kindergarten. I remember everyone making a fuss over the fact that we were the class of 2000. It was a big event! At the start of first grade we were in a new apartment and I was at a new school. Halfway through the year we moved again and I started as a new student in another school. I had barely been in school for two years and I had already attended three different schools. If we kept this up, I would become quite the world traveler!

Before I start this next chapter, I feel it is important to mention again how very thankful I am for the life-altering relationships I have formed through the sometimes vindictive behavior of my mother. This is the point in the story where you, the reader, begin to truly understand the complex mind of my mother. In the pages to come, there will be times of confusion along with moments of sheer disgust. For this reason, it is important to remember that, for me, the result of all the negatives is a life of no regrets. I am the person I have grown to be because of every moment in my life. I would change nothing and ask no sympathy for any of the disappointing experiences.

Optimism and faith have been my motivation for as far back as I can recall. To everyone who has contributed to this intensely character-building life, I give you my heart. Thank you for loving me despite my situation and standing by me in the darkest of hours. Parts of me are parts of you, grown from the love you've so graciously shared. I love you more than words can express.

Chapter Two

My First Stepfather

Mom met Kerry in the summer of 1988. They worked together for an assisted living service for the mentally ill. Kerry was a house manager at one of the residences and my mother at another. He was only nineteen years old and dating his high school sweetheart. He was more than six feet tall and I loved when he put me on his shoulders so I could see the world! My mother, claiming to be twenty-eight (she was really thirty-one), was dating a much shorter bearded man at the time. He was always nice to me, but he wasn't very kid-friendly. The only real memory I have of him is running into their bedroom during a thunderstorm and seeing him in my mom's underwear! I ran right back to my bedroom!

Most of the time my mother and I lived with the same three mentally disabled people. There was a women named Erin, who was a schizophrenic. I didn't know what that meant at the time, but I remember her telling me that it was really important that she take her medication. When we first moved in, Erin would try to hide her pills in her pillow instead of taking them. According to my mother she came walking into her room one night with a butcher's knife and held it over her head! She kept a much closer eye on her after that. At least, that is what she told me when the fear she had just unleashed became evident in my eyes. It must have been true, though, because Erin always seemed normal enough to me.

There was an older man named Orin. He didn't say much but I remember that he would always pick his nose, roll the boogers in a ball, and flick them across the room. Occasionally, he would have a "fit" at the dinner table and my mother would yell, "Everybody clear the room, Orin's going to blow!"

He would get all riled up, wave his index finger around in circles, and start throwing anything he could get his hands on. We lost plates, silverware, you name it! My mother was usually able to calm him down soon after that, and he would go back to picking his nose and flicking it across the room.

Then there was the most interesting of the three. I can't recall her name, but she was a handful! Once, we were kicked out of a department store because she flipped out and started banging on the glass case where all the jewelry was stored. My mother sent me outside with Erin and we waited for what seemed like forever. Once they made it outside, the lady got into someone else's car and wouldn't get out. My mother screamed at her, but she wouldn't budge. The owners of the car, a man and a woman, walked up to find my mother yelling at what appeared to be an empty backseat. I bet they thought she was crazy! By the time they made it up to the car and realized what was going on, she had jumped out and ran to where I was standing. My mother apologized to the very lost-looking couple and shuffled all of us into our car. We lived with these folks at a few different places and it was always entertaining.

Over time, my mother and Kerry grew close and eventually broke off their current relationships to be with each other. Young and naïve, my mother had Kerry wrapped around her little finger. At this moment in his life, he longed for independence and saw a life with us as just what he had been searching for. He plunged in headfirst and didn't look back.

In the early stages of their relationship we lived in many different places around Pennsylvania. There was the small apartment where we shared our first Christmas and a neat little lake house in the Poconos. In the beginning I loved it, but I remember at some points feeling very jealous of him. I wasn't used to sharing my mother with anyone. For the last five years it had been just us, so this was a big adjustment for me. An adjustment I grew very thankful I had to make.

Kerry's mother was never a fan of my mother. I think she may have had some inclination that she was not what she seemed. When he told her he planned to marry my mother, she was furious, even more so when she found out it was to happen in just a few weeks. Despite her discontent, Kerry's mother still attended the ceremony. Although she made it very clear that she did not approve. Before the justice of the peace started the ceremony, she asked him (very loudly) if he would be reading the part where he asks if anyone objects, because for his reference, she did!

I was also not on my best behavior that day. Likely due to the feelings of jealously I mentioned earlier. Anyway, I decided it would be funny to ruin every picture taken that day. The best photo we have is of the three of us with me front and center with my fist in front of my face. Boy was I precious. I wouldn't have blamed Kerry for having second thoughts!

And So the Travels Begin . . .

Eventually I adjusted and became more than content with our new family. Kerry was no longer my stepdad; he was just my dad. Looking back, I can only imagine how hard it must have been for him. My mother was in control of the money, which meant we never had any! Yet miraculously a large sum would always appear when we needed it. She told my dad that my godmother or another relative was helping out. Somehow, we always seemed to manage.

Shortly after the wedding, we moved from our apartment to the lake house in the Poconos. It was summer then and my mother only worked part-time. Which meant there were many days where we were able to hang out at the house together all day. In the mornings, my mother would make everyone breakfast and plan out her activities for the day. As soon as we were finished, my mother turned on the television and for the remainder of the day we would watch "our shows" (as we referred to them) while my mother tended to her "to do" list of the day and I played. Our favorite show was *I Love Lucy*. My mother loved Lucille Ball and had introduced her to me at a very young age. I quickly became a fan! It was on a day that spring when we were in the middle of our normal routine that we heard the news of Ms. Ball's death. We were both in the living room watching our shows. My mother was ironing and I was pretending I worked at a library with a stack of books and my new stamp set when the news channel anchors broke into our program. Both of us froze, refusing to believe it. Without taking her eyes off the television set, my mother walked slowly over to the couch where I was sitting. Still holding Kerry's dress shirt in her hands, she slumped onto the cushion. Within seconds, her face was buried in his shirt and she was crying incessantly. Not knowing what to do, I threw my arms around her and joined in with her sobbing. I guess you could say this was my first experience dealing with the loss of someone. Granted, we were not close relatives of hers, but she meant something to us both, as silly as that may seem to some.

We also watched a great deal of *Little House on the Prairie*. With my long brown hair and freckles, I resembled Melissa Gilbert's character, Laura, quite a bit growing up, so my mother gave me one of her nicknames used on the show: Half-pint. Another character on the show, Mr. Edwards, reminded me of my godfather. Mostly because they both sported a lumberjack beard and his relationship with Laura on the show was much like that of mine with my godfather. All those similarities were very comforting to me.

At some point we decided to move to New England. In Concord, New Hampshire, my mother found an agency similar to the one they currently worked for, and very shortly after that we relocated. We had recently adopted a beautiful collie, Nicholas. He wasn't the most intelligent dog, but he was very sweet and loving. I would lay on my stomach in front of the television and he would lay on my back. We still had both of our cats, Ashley and Shadow. Sadly, after we moved, Ashley started urinating on my bed immediately after my mother had washed the sheets, so eventually we had to give her away. Shadow was most definitely my cat. He was honestly the coolest cat I have ever had. I would dress him up in doll clothes and push him around the house in my baby buggy. He was such a good sport! We named him Shadow because when he was a kitten he followed me everywhere; plus he was mostly gray, with little white paws.

My mother found an amazing log cabin for us to rent on a beautiful lake in Bradford, New Hampshire. There was a small private beach in our front yard and a wooded area in the back. The inside was fully furnished and had hardwood floors that Nicky would slide on every time he darted into the house. He was usually stopped by a piece of furniture or the wall!

Bradford was a true example of small-town New England. Their drive to work took an hour through woods and mountains, which became challenging. Since my mother and Kerry were both working, I began going to a nice in-home day care. The woman who ran it had it set up with a giant fake tree in the middle of the house that I used to climb on when I wasn't helping her take care of the younger children. I only went for a short time. Eventually, my mother and Kerry grew to hate their jobs and decided to quit. She told him they would be fine because someone was sending money to help us out. She was still in control of the bills and always seemed to have it covered, so neither of us worried.

That is until one day when two men showed up with a tow truck and told us they had to take my dad's car. My mother made up a story to cover the reasoning for the repossession and, as I would later find out, revealed that she had been lying about her true identity because of some dark secret she had been holding back from him about her family.

Everything began to go downhill after that. We were broke and the mysterious money that had been rolling in before, suddenly stopped. There was a public assistance program in the town that issued us a grant to pay our rent for a few months, but what we would do after that was unknown. Not knowing what else to do, Kerry decided to join the Air Force.

He could not begin his service right away, however. Delayed entry meant that we had to wait six months before he would start testing and training. Our resources exhausted at this point, my mother suggested we move to Florida where she had been in contact with a dear friend who could help us get settled until Kerry was enlisted. Now down to one car, with only enough room for our necessities, we were also forced to say goodbye to Nicholas. This was heartbreaking for all of us, well at least Kerry and myself. My mother never seemed to have a problem leaving behind animals. She was never cruel to them and would never leave them without someone to care for them, but she also didn't seem to dwell on their absence.

When we arrived in Florida, there was no friend waiting for us and no place for us to stay. We ended up in Cocoa Beach where we rented a trailer just across the highway from the ocean. My dad wasn't scheduled to enter the Air Force until April 1990 and it was only November 1989. So he quickly took a job as a cook at a very popular fast food restaurant and my mother started her own cleaning company. Knowing what I now do about my mother, the cleaning business was maniacally genius on her part. Sure, she would clean your house, but she would also snag a few blank checks in the process to clean out your bank account later.

That year, it was the coldest winter on record in Florida. All sorts of records were broken in temperature and snowfall. There were rolling blackouts across the state and residents were unable to leave the city due to ice-covered bridges, which was virtually unheard of in Florida!

That Christmas Eve, we were without power and we all had to snuggle on the couch to keep warm. There was a gas stove in the trailer that gave off some heat and allowed my dad to cook his Christmas goose for the three of us. It was a bit slimy, but it was good.

Early in February, Kerry received an odd call at work from his brother. He was with his mother who told him that someone had cashed the check she sent him for his birthday for $1,500.00 instead of $50.00. She was told that the bank would not cover the discrepancy unless she pressed charges against the perpetrator. Knowing the perpetrator was most likely my mother, she chose not to and instead paid all the fees herself. When a copy of the check was sent to him later, he said that my mother had crossed out everything on the check and rewritten it in her own handwriting. It is crazy to think that anyone would have accepted something so obviously forged, but my mother has a gift of getting people to do what she wants. Even if her request is ridiculous.

In April, Kerry left for basic training in Texas. The plan was to wait for him in Florida and then meet him wherever he ended up being stationed, but about halfway through basic training we lost contact.

Surprise!

After basic training, Kerry was shipped to Fort Benjamin Harrison in Indianapolis, Indiana. Much to his shock and utter relief when he landed, my mother and I were there to meet him at the gate. She had told him she decided to rent a truck and move the both of us up there as a surprise! She continued to explain that our lack of communication was due to the run-in we had along the way when someone had stolen our moving truck and left us stranded. The only things she was lucky enough to save were my dad's stereo and television. Apparently these items were in the car we were driving while the moving truck was left at the hotel. The real story was quite a bit less dramatic. My mother had actually sold, pawned, or thrown away all of our possessions that wouldn't fit in the car. She then packed us up and drove from Florida to Illinois to spend time with her parents. We rented a small apartment in a little town outside of Chicago and I vaguely remember attending school for a few weeks until there was a blowout between my mother and her parents. We stopped by their house one day and they began yelling at her about a check she wrote and money she owed them. My mother didn't have a bank account that I knew of, and at that point I had learned that it was better not to ask.

After the fight, she left me with my grandparents for several weeks. I later found out that she had forged one of their checks and was arrested. They told me she would be back soon, but it didn't matter to me at the time. I hardly ever saw my grandparents and they spoiled me rotten! They were both retired, so we were always together doing fun projects around the house. My grandfather spent many days making wooden lawn ornaments for my grandmother and me to paint. I was in heaven!

As soon as my mother was released, we left for Indiana . . .

South Dakota

Kerry believed my mother's tragic tale, partly because he was just plan happy to see us and have the family back together! My mother and I rented a small apartment off the base where we stayed while he attended school. It was summer and there were a lot of other kids who lived in the complex with us, so I was always outside. At night, my mother would let me stay up and watch movies with her until I fell asleep on the couch. I had a bedroom, but I never slept in it! It was basically storage for my toys, which had dwindled quite a bit since the "stolen" moving truck incident. When we lived in Florida I could barely fit in my bed due to the number of stuffed animals I shared it with. When we left, I was allowed to bring two boxes and whatever I could carry.

When my dad graduated, we packed up again and moved to Rapid City, South Dakota. His first assignment was to be at Ellsworth Air Force Base. When we arrived, it was in the fall of 1990 and the city was filled with smoke from the recent forest fires. It was kind of spooky, like something out of a horror film. The air was thick and smelled of soot, but the landscape was amazing.

Just after we were settled, Kerry and mom started fighting a lot more than usual. One night, he came home and immediately confronted my mother. Apparently, my father being in the service expedited the leads in law enforcement that were tracking her and when the numerous checks she wrote at the PX in Fort Ben began bouncing, it was only a matter of time before my father was being questioned by his chief master sergeant. When he came home to confront her, she denied everything.

The next morning, she acted like nothing had happened. She rushed my father off to work and kissed him goodbye. She made me breakfast and plopped me down in front of the television as a distraction to her erratic behavior. As I finished my cereal, my mother was strategically packing up our necessities and loading them into the car. By the time I noticed what was happening, she was already rushing me to get to the car.

Looking at her with objection, she stopped me before I could say anything.

"You know it is the only way . . . don't you?" she said as she grazed my lower lip with her finger.

Tears welled up in my eyes as I turned my head in confused disagreement.

I knew my objection wouldn't matter. We were leaving whether I wanted to or not.

"Baby, it's time." She spoke in a soft voice. "We have to leave."

I said nothing; all I could do was nod.

I made my way toward the car, making every effort to stay as far from my mother as possible even though I knew the closeness of the journey would be inescapable. I opened the passenger door and lifted my almost lifeless body into the oversized seat. I closed the door and turned myself to face the window. My mother entered shortly after and not a word was said. I drifted to sleep, knowing I would wake up miles away from my life, but hoping it was a dream just the same.

I woke up to the sound of a chipper young fellow in the drive-thru lane. "Would you like one or two of the dolls?" he said.

"Two!" I heard my mother specify. "Baby, I got you two of those dolls you wanted and a hash brown."

I looked over. Her eyes were filled with regret, and the fear that I would see through her nice gesture.

"Thanks Mom." I said in a soft mumble.

Just like that, we took off.

Chapter 3

The Accident

I heard sirens screaming as I tried to focus. Eventually, I was able to make out red flashing lights bouncing on what was left of the passenger window. I was surrounded by fire trucks and ambulances. I remember trying to move my body or make a sound, but there was nothing. As I restored focus on the flashing red lights, everything went dark.

In the next moment of consciousness, my head had slumped over and all I was able to see was the blood that marked my body. I was immediately flooded with an overwhelming sense of fear, and the lines between dream and reality began to blur. I could hear a loud screeching sound to my right, but was unable to move to see what it was. I knew something was happening next to me, but my vision was still too blurry to make out what it was. I could somewhat feel my body now, but only enough to realize that I was being moved?!

As the paramedic pulled me from the crumpled car, I kept focus on the place where I had been pinned just moments before, and then I noticed it! The slipper I had been wearing at the time of the crash. The black-and-white pattern that had once resembled the head of a friendly cow, was now just blood-soaked fabric covered in matted cotton. *My grandma gave me those,* I thought, as I rested my head on the shoulder of my hero. He carried me to the ambulance and laid me onto the stretcher. My mother and godmother came aboard behind me and sat down next to my left side. My mother was hysterical, and rightfully so. I tried to move my left arm in her direction, but nothing happened. I looked over to see my arm lying limp next to me as my shoulder joint moved slightly. Able to move my head now, I anxiously looked down at my legs. Both of them were covered in blood and on the right one, I could see the bone. The pain set in and I began to shake.

"It's okay, sweetie," the paramedic said to me as he gently pushed my head down and looked into my eyes. "We're going to fix you right up!"

Just then, two other paramedics jumped into the vehicle and began cutting my nightgown. I screamed! To them it was just a piece of clothing, but to someone in my situation, it was a familiarity I needed to lean on. My mother was hysterical and I was terrified. I needed something.

Thankfully, the paramedic who lifted me from the vehicle came to the rescue again. He had retrieved a very important stuffed animal from our crushed car. When my mother and I left Kerry in South Dakota, I took with me a stuffed cat he had given to me. The paramedic handed it over, and I clung to it for dear life.

"I thought he would make you feel better," he said as I clutched it with my still-working right arm. This was enough, and I no longer objected to the slicing apart of my favorite nightgown.

All I remember of the trip to the hospital is the pain. Every bump intensified the excruciating throbbing in my right leg. Eventually it was just too much and I passed out.

I woke up in the emergency room as my godmother was removing my earrings and my mother was placing my rescue cat, now equipped with a hospital ID card, next to my side.

"He's going to go into surgery with you, sweetie," she said.

They both whispered "I love you" and I was wheeled away.

Hours later, I woke up screaming! I was hoping it was all a dream; and all I wanted was my mom. She jumped up to come to my rescue from a cot they had placed next to my bed, and held me so tightly I could hardly breathe.

"It's okay baby, you're okay. I'm here and everything is going to be okay. Get some sleep."

The next morning my mother woke me to say she was going back to the apartment to take a shower, but that she would come back that evening.

I had to stay in the hospital for a very long time, and boy did that clock move slowly. Thankfully, my right leg was still there, healing from a compound fracture. I could still use my right hand for writing, although it was a little annoying with the IV sticking out of my hand. They couldn't put it in my left arm because my collarbone had been broken from the force of the blow to the passenger's-side door and was now in a sling. Apparently, at the time of the impact, my left arm had been wedged between the seats. My right leg had been between the seat and the door, hence most of the damage was there. I had a cast up to my knee with a little window that opened up to clean the wound. That always grossed me out, but I just looked away when they changed the dressings. It was weird.

My hospital sentence lasted about a month, but I had lots of visitors to help pass the time. Kerry even flew in from South Dakota and brought me a huge teddy bear! After the accident, he had received a call from a cop who had my mother handcuffed to a chair next to him. The cop had arrested my mother, and was trying to figure out who my mother and I were. Kerry connected him with the FBI agent he was working with in

South Dakota. The cop gave him the details about the accident and told him which hospital I was staying in. Thankfully, he was able work through the military to get a voucher from the Red Cross to fly to Pennsylvania. He wasn't able to stay too long, but I was glad he was there.

I had not seen my godparents, Maryellen and John, for a long time before the crash. Mom and I had moved away shortly after she had married Kerry and we had little contact with them for about a year or so. There was a letter here and there from us to them, but they were never very informative.

Then, just a few days before the accident happened, we had shown up at their house for trick-or-treating. Needless to say, they were very surprised! I remember feeling glad to see them and their children, who also came to keep me company during my hospital stay. We all played games, watched movies, and talked in those few days before disaster struck.

Funny thing though . . . my mother never came back.

I asked everyone why my mother had not returned to the hospital and they said she was sick, too, and had a room in another hospital. She was getting better, just like I was. I knew my mother had ridden in the ambulance with me to the hospital with Maryellen, because I remember them both taking my earrings out just before they rushed me into surgery. My mother had given me the stuffed cat that the EMT had retrieved from the wreck, who wore a hospital band around his neck. The nurse told me he needed it so that he would be allowed in the operating room with me.

My mother was also there when I first woke up from surgery. I woke up frightened and confused, immediately yelling for my mother, and she was there. The next day she told me she was going home to shower and change clothes, and bring me some of my toys for my long hospital stay. She never returned. So it seemed reasonable to me that something may have happened to her after she left. Maybe some of her injuries came later or something.

The day finally came for me to go home! I was so excited. The doctor said I would still be in a wheelchair for some time, but that eventually the cast would come off and my arm would be out of the sling. I was told that my mother was still in the hospital so, in the meantime, I would go to live with my godparents. I was going to share a room with their daughter—who I now wholeheartedly consider my sister—until my mom was able to come and take me home.

My New Home

L ife at my godparents' house was great! I had a brother and sister to play with, and a mother and father that I considered my own. Being a single mother, when mom and I were together, she didn't always have time to entertain me. It was a nice change to always have something to do and someone with whom to do it. It was also a great distraction from the crazy events I had just experienced, and the lingering question: *Where is my mom . . . ?*

I was still unable to move around very well by myself, so my godfather installed an intercom next to my bed in case I had to pee during the night. I remember one time I buzzed him and said, "I have to pee."

After I buzzed several more times, he replied, "How bad do you have to go?"

I paused—actually thinking about it—and replied, "Bad enough to try and crawl if I have to."

A few minutes later, still chuckling, John entered the bedroom. He picked me up and carried me to the bathroom, waiting outside the door for a signal that he may return me to bed and go back to his peaceful slumber.

"You told me to buzz," I said as he set me back in bed.

He kissed me on the forehead and smiled. "I know . . . good night."

It sucked being so dependent on someone else all the time and sometimes I would try to hold it for as long as I could so I didn't have to wake him up.

I missed my mom, but a part of me was enjoying living in this new home, with this new family. I always felt so loved. There was a security in this house and with my godparents. There always has been.

Looking back in my life, the first memory I can recall is of John. I must have been barely three years old. I remember him strumming on his guitar and softly singing as I attempted, with my young innocent voice, to accompany him. We sang songs like "There Was an Old Lady Who Swallowed a Fly" and those I am most fond of: "Lady" and "Lucille." To this day those songs make me feel warm and fuzzy inside. I always felt so secure and wanted when he was near. I never had to question his love or fear he would leave me. I am sure to this day he still has no idea how much it means to me to make him proud and have him close.

Christmas

My godparents lived in the Pocono Mountains in an old stone house set back in the woods. I had always thought of the house as something out of a fairy tale, surrounded by majestic trees with ivy covering the sides of the house. The backyard was huge, and next to the garage was a Concord grapevine that produced the most deliciously mouthwatering purple morsels each year. Pine trees lined the property, and a small creek ran along the left side of the house and down the mountain.

Christmastime, as you can imagine, was like something right out of a holiday movie. The living room was filled with the smell of pine from the enormous freshly cut tree in the corner. Next to the tree was the piano, where my godmother played

Christmas songs for us while we decorated the tree. I remember feeling an array of emotions as I sat back and took in the view of my new reality. I was overjoyed to be surrounded by loved ones, but a part of me was heartbroken to realize that this was the first Christmas that I could remember without my mother. I was angry at her for being untruthful, but I still missed her.

My godmother must have known this moment may come, because unbeknownst to me, she had retrieved some of my mother's Christmas ornaments from the apartment when I was in the hospital. And in this moment of overwhelming emotion, she stopped playing the piano and brought me a white shirt box from upstairs. As she handed it to me, I noticed my mother's handwriting on the label: CHRISTMAS ORNAMENTS. Knowing immediately what the box contained, my eyes welled up with tears as I jumped up and squeezed her as tight as I could. She hugged me back and kissed my head. I felt safe.

Wait . . . What?

Even though life was really great at my godparents' house, I thought about my mom a lot. Eventually, I started to doubt the story about her being in the hospital; it just didn't match up. We were never able to visit her, she never wrote, and I was never able to call her when I wanted to. Whenever I voiced these concerns, the answers were very vague. They never acted as if they were trying to deceive me but more like my questions made them uncomfortable, and they were quick to change the subject.

Then one night, after dinner, Maryellen and John took me into the kitchen to talk. For a while, they just stared at me with long serious gazes.

Until, in a low comforting voice, John looked at me and said, "Tiff, honey, we need to talk to you about your mom."

Just then I felt something click. I looked up at them and said, "She's not in the hospital is she?"

"No . . ." Maryellen replied. "She's in jail."

Oddly, somehow I wasn't surprised. I never remembered her being in jail before, but it still didn't seem to startle me at all. However, what they told me next knocked me on the ground.

First they explained that my mother had left me at the hospital and arrived at our apartment to be met by the police and arrested on several charges. My godparents stepped up as my foster parents and I was then placed in their care. All of these arrangements had been made during my close-to-a-month-long recovery in the hospital. Completely under my nose and at no time did they ever let on that something was amiss? That is strength in its truest form.

After it was clear that I had grasped this, they went on to explain how there was a bit more to my mother than she let on. Quite a bit more actually. Turns out my mother, the neglected youth, has not one but two sets of parents. I am not sure why, but it never seemed odd to me before, maybe because most kids have two sets of grandparents, and up until that point I had only seen either set a handful of times. I never really gave much thought to the idea that they were all her parents. I knew that they all lived in Illinois. We never saw both sets at the same time, but outside of that I had not given it any thought.

Here is where it gets crazy.

Maryellen and John explained to me that my mother had been adopted when she was very young by the cousin of her birth mother. The details of which have always been a bit fuzzy for everyone. There are several stories and I don't know if anyone, aside from those involved, really knows the truth. What we do know is that Mom was the only one given away out of six children. Her adoptive mother was not able to have children, but she wanted them desperately. Her and her husband adopted my mother when she was two. They always told me it was because she had an eye condition that her biological parents could not afford to fix, so they offered to adopt her because they could. There are other versions of this story, but no one really knows which to believe. Regardless of what is true or false in the case of her adoption, it is clear that the entire situation did a number on her psyche.

On September 18, two days after my tenth birthday, my mom was deemed by the courts as an unfit mother. So, when she was done serving time, she was going to be released into the custody of her adoptive parents. In addition to this, she was granting them custody of me when she was released. This meant I had to leave. I had to leave and go live with people I barely knew.

I slumped down in my chair and went over everything in my head. At the time, I thought it was the worst news, but I tried to focus on the positive. At least I would get to see my mom soon. She would be held in a facility close to my grandparents' house until her release and that meant we could go visit. I didn't care if it was in a jail; it would just be nice to see her.

Maryellen and John reassured me that I would still have a little time with them before I had to leave, and I was starting to warm up to the idea of a new adventure, until they told me the rest.

After my mom was arrested, her entire cover was blown. As it turns out she had been on the run since before I was born. She went AWOL from the Army and then left for New York sometime in 1980. Shortly before I was born she met a woman whose identity she stole and had been using up until her recent unfortunate incarceration.

She had been operating under a completely different identity for the last ten years. The name we all knew her by and the name on my birth certificate belonged to a totally different person. Not only was she several years older than I thought, but apparently her birthday was in August instead of October. I was learning my mother's name for the first time. At this point, I was speechless.

Chapter 4

The Identity Crisis

Why my mother left each time she did was never entirely clear, but who she was running from was evident in every move she made. For my mother, identity theft wasn't just something she did to get by, it was who she was. Running away from herself became a psychological ritual, cleansing the sins of a previous life and starting a new one. Until time ran out, money ran scarce, and her story ran thin. Then it was on to the next.

Turns out she had been doing this for years. It was much easier back then. There was a time when one's social security number was listed right on identification cards. Steal someone's driver's license and you have a whole new life. Which then allowed for a whole new line of credit. Many would find this to be heartless, but to her, she was entitled somehow; she believed the person owed her!

Now that her cover had been completely blown, I began to learn more and more about the life my mother had led before she had assumed the identity I had always known. The spotty recollections of my childhood started to make more sense.

I don't recall my mother talking about her life growing up much, just that she felt her adoptive parents didn't really understand her and they needed to go their separate ways. They lived in northern Illinois, as did her biological parents, and we had visited them both several times in the past when we had gone missing from our other life. I guess I never really noticed them calling her by another name. More than likely she had given me an excuse I had no reason not to believe, so I just disregarded it.

With this new information, I began to understand where all of my mother's and my random road trips fit into the picture. When we left Florida in 1990, we spent several months in Illinois before we met my stepdad in Indiana. I realized now that the grandparents I met on this visit were my mother's adoptive parents. They were both retired and lived in a two-story yellow house on a corner lot behind a large Methodist church in Roscoe, Illinois. My grandfather Alden was a marvel at woodworking and spent a great deal of his free time making yard ornaments and bird houses. When we first arrived, I had come down with whooping cough and my grandmother Katherine suggested my mother give me the old home remedy of brandy and applesauce to cure the problem. Sure enough, I choked it down, and amazingly it went away after a few days (at least that is what my mother tells me). We didn't stay for long. Which I later learned was because she ended up stealing some of my grandparents' checks. They didn't call the police, but we must have taken off as soon as they confronted her about it.

According to Kerry, we returned to South Dakota after that. His mother had flown out to help him deal with my mother's aftermath. When we arrived, my mother hid me somewhere and went back to him, begging him to go AWOL and run away with us! He refused and she took off to Pennsylvania. I was shocked to find out later that she had actually managed to steal two cars while we were living in Florida. This was one of the many discoveries that Kerry made while working with attorneys in Rapid City to divorce my mother, return the stolen merchandise, and declare bankruptcy.

I also learned that during the last week we were in South Dakota, my mother ran one last bank scheme to be sure we would have enough money for our travels. She made a deposit through the ATM at her bank in South Dakota for $3,000.00 with an empty envelope. She repeated this action several times, totaling an estimated $8,700.00 in false funds; $5,345.00 of which was then withdrawn shortly after at different locations.

These activities were included on the list of charges she was arrested for after the accident.

My stepdad did not hear from us until my godmother called and told him about the car accident. He arranged emergency funding from the Red Cross to be able to come to Pennsylvania to visit me in the hospital, but was only able to stay for a few days. He looked into possibly adopting me, but was told that unfortunately, he held no legal rights. He felt good knowing I would be with my godparents; they were like parents to me and they were nothing if they were not honest, loving, and loyal.

Once in a while he would hear from the FBI and they would tell him about the different people my mother had scammed, including some of the people who caught her. Apparently they were pretty amazed by her talents.

Feeling at Home

My godparents lived in a beautiful two-story stone house in the country. A house that was very familiar to me and felt more like home than any other place I had ever lived. The entire family accepted me with open arms and the family community of our church was another comfort I had come to rely on. Given the mind-blowing reveal of my mother's alternate life, familiarity was just what I needed to move on.

I stayed in contact with my mother. She would write me letters from jail and every once in a while I was able to talk to her on the phone or visit with her. I remember always asking her to French braid my hair while we talked and I would keep it in as long as I could before it began to look like I had bedhead.

My godmother made sure to pay special attention to keeping it looking presentable until I was ready to take it out. She knew it was my way of coping with my mother's absence and she never questioned it.

Needless to say, life with a cast was not very fun. It remained on my leg for several months after my release from the hospital. For the first few months I was not able to use crutches, because my collarbone was still healing, so I navigated my way around in a wheelchair. At first I thought it was neat, but it grew old very fast. I was not able to get it wet, so bath time was a bit more challenging than usual, but I was in good hands. My godmother would wrap my leg with a garbage bag and as long as I propped it up on the side of the tub, it was business as usual. I wasn't able to walk up the stairs, either, but there was always someone there to carry me to my destination. Their son, who I refer to now as my brother, rescued me from the insane amount of itching by suggesting I slide a ruler into my cast to scratch my leg to give me some bit of relief. I remember thinking he was a genius!

Perhaps my least favorite part was what I like to call "the tiny window of death." It was a small square in the middle of my cast that was cut on three sides so it opened like a window to reveal the large wound on my leg where the doctors had fused my bones back together. It was disgusting! I refused to look at it for the longest time until my godmother asked me to try and change my own dressing. She thought it would be good for me and I didn't blame her for trying. She had been doing it every day since I had left the hospital. I remember opening the little window to see what looked like someone's mouth sewn shut with barbed wire. I am sure it wasn't that bad, but that is how I remembered it. I immediately freaked out and started bawling. My godmother felt horrible for suggesting it, even though I was just being a wussy about it all. That poor woman; what a saint! The sacrifices everyone made for me will never be forgotten.

Living with a Cast

For the first few months I was home from the hospital, I did my school work remotely. My godfather traveled a lot for his job and my godmother worked during the day as the manager of a crisis pregnancy center, so I spent most of the day with different friends of the family. Mostly members of our church and people I had known when I was younger.

I enjoyed my time with all of them. It was always different. Since I was still not yet able to attend regular classes, sometimes I would be the only kid, like when I was able to stay with Holly. I loved staying with Holly! She and her husband and their two children, among others, had taken my mother and me in when we first came to the church after I was born. They too lived in a picturesque stone house in the Pocono Mountains and it always had the aroma of a freshly lit fire. Holly was extremely artistic and always creating something or working on a project. Either way, she would always find a way for me to participate, and I always looked forward to spending time with her.

I struggled with my inability to move freely and would often get frustrated because I was not able to do the activities I was used to. Holly helped me to find new activities that I was able to do regardless of my situation. I would practice drawing by looking at an object and sketching it out slowly on a sheet of blank paper. Glancing back and forth from the object to the paper, until it began to resemble the object in question. When I grew bored of that, we would play a card game or make a craft. She helped me to stay positive in an otherwise negative time in my life.

I also stayed with my godmother's friend Celeste, who cared for several other children as well. She loaded us up with activities to keep everyone occupied. We played board games, made crafts for our parents, and built castles out of blocks in the playroom. Every day we had something different and fun to snack on and, when it snowed, she would bundle us all up and let us play outside. For me that meant wrapping my cast in plastic and trying to cram it into a pair of snow pants! Looking back now, I don't know where she found the energy. Celeste was very understanding and attentive to my needs. She helped me with my homework and always made sure I had everything

I needed. She also attended our church with her husband and their two children. Her daughter was very good friends with my godsister, so this was again a place where I felt very comfortable.

I continued to keep in touch with my mother during this time with letters and occasional visits. Kerry also kept in touch with me. He would call me from time to time, and we wrote letters back and forth. For a very short time, my mother had fabricated a story about being pregnant with his daughter when she was arrested. I remember her telling me that I would have a baby sister named Tia, but when I asked her about it later she said she had lost the baby. Kerry later told me that he had requested that she provide proof of her pregnancy and she never responded.

Freedom!

The day finally came when it was time for my cast to be removed! By this point my collarbone had healed and I was pushing my boundaries walking on my leg. The bottom of my cast was starting to show evidence of my readiness to take the next step in my recovery. My godmother took me to my appointment and boy was I glad she was there. As the doctor explained the procedure, my excitement turned into fear. Then he pulled out the saw that he would be using to cut the cast.

I was convinced that he was going to make a mistake and cut me. They both reassured me that the saw would not cut my skin, and the doctor even showed me by placing it against his hand. I was still leery, but I allowed him to proceed. I clung to my godmother with all my might as the doctor prepared my cast for removal. As the saw screeched on, I buried my head in her lap and cried.

When he was finished, I lifted my head to see a very shriveled version of what I remembered to be my leg. I still had stitches, but the wound did not look as terrifying as I had remembered when viewing it through the "tiny window of death." They fitted me with an air splint and sent me on my way. It would be a long road to recovery, but I was ready!

Chapter 5

Ready, Set, Sled!

H aving the air splint instead of the cast was great, but eventually I grew tired of constantly having to squeeze it under my pants and the inability to move freely. For the first time in months I was finally able to run around on my own and I couldn't wait to enjoy it! I was a bit wobbly at first and my newfound siblings picked on me for it, but it was all in good fun. They included me in their activities as much as they could.

One day, after a fresh snowfall, we all decided to go sledding on one of the hills near our house. I geared up in my pink snowsuit and the new hat, gloves, and snow boots I had gotten for Christmas. My siblings did the same and we headed out for a day of fun! We were equipped with three sleds. My brother was dragging the family's wooden toboggan, and my sister and I each had the traditional plastic circle sleds. We trucked up the mountain and slid down time and again until I grew tired and refused to continue. My siblings taunted me for a bit until I agreed to go down one more time. We decided to take the toboggan this time because we could all ride it at the same time. My brother sat in front, then my sister, then myself. We sent our other sleds down the hill and prepared for our journey to meet them. My brother launched the "Ready, Set, Go!" and in a flash we were off!

Halfway down the hill we hit an ice patch and the sled flew off the path and into the trees. As the sled came to a halt, my leg slammed directly into the trunk of a sapling. I screamed in pain! My sister turned to see what had happened and found me a blubbering mess beside her.

"I think I broke my leg!" I cried out to her.

Before she could respond, my brother chimed in, "Oh come on, no you didn't!"

They pulled the sled away from me and my sister tried pulling me out of the snow, but I screamed in agony.

"Tiffany, there is no way you could have broken your leg. Don't you have your splint on?" my sister said, trying to reason with me.

I looked up at her and shook my head.

Her expression immediately shifted to show the gravity of this new information. They stared at each other for a moment and then leaped into action. My brother grabbed the sled and brought it back over to where I was sitting. My sister motioned for me to put my arm around her neck as she stood beside me and, in one fell swoop, she lifted me as my brother slid the sled under my body. My sister made sure I was safely aboard and they pulled me back to the house.

My godmother was waiting with hot cocoa, thinking we would be needing it after our fun-filled day of sledding and was sadly disappointed by a much-needed trip to the hospital. She still blames herself for not checking to see that I had my air splint on, but that is in no way justified. I was a sneaky kid and decided not to wear my splint even though I knew I needed to. I was wearing snow pants for goodness' sake!

I did rebreak my leg, although it was a very minor break compared to what I'd experienced in the accident. I was sent home with crutches and I was back on track in a few months!

Easter

My godparents were always planning fun events for us to do as a family. One Easter, they hid plastic eggs around the yard for us kids to find. Only they didn't contain candy, but letters: DWLNSYEORID. We were told that we were to organize the letters to reveal our Easter present! They stood back and watched as we worked diligently to determine what the letters spelled. If it had not been for my brother and sister, we would have never figured it out.

Finally, my brother said in an unsure voice, "Desiny . . . world?"

My sister then exclaimed, "DISNEY WORLD!"

We all paused and looked at our parents for confirmation . . .

They both smiled and yelled, "You got it!"

Everyone screamed and all three of us kids grabbed hold of each other and jumped around the room screaming!

The trip was any kid's dream and we couldn't wait to go!

We did not have to wait long; before we knew it we were on the plane and ready to depart. My godparents had rented a condo in Disney for five days and every day was jam-packed with activities. They bought an autograph book for each of us kids at the beginning of the trip, and I remember feeling what could only be described as starstruck. I could not wait to start filling up the pages!

We started our vacation itinerary early the next morning and I mean really early. We were all too excited to sleep and once we finally drifted into dreamland it was not very long before we were leaping out of bed, ready for our adventure to begin! We strapped on our fanny packs filled with snacks and extra pens (for our autographs) and headed out the door!

The first Disney character we ran into was Pluto. He was dancing around the front entrance as we were walking in. I looked toward my godmother for approval to run to him and before she finished nodding I was sprinting toward the first famous person I had ever met! I threw my arms around him and buried my face in his fluffy orange fur. I squeezed him as tight as I could, still managing to clutch my autograph book in one hand. As I stepped back, I managed to get out "Sir, may I please have your autograph?"

Grinning ear to ear, I held out the book as far as my little arm would extend and stared up at him. As I handed it over to him, I dug through my fanny pack looking for a pen. I remember hoping that I stumbled upon a marker first. He might have trouble grasping a tiny pen with his paws, I thought, and I didn't want him to be embarrassed. Luckily, I found a chunky red marker. Satisfied with my find I handed it over and watched as my blank book of pages received its first signature!

As the day went on the autographs piled up. Most of the time the lines were short, but the line for the Teenage Mutant Ninja Turtle characters was not. This would be four in one, so we didn't mind waiting. About halfway through the line, my sister and I smelled something weird. We looked around to try and locate the source of the odor and came upon our brother . . . his lips were blue! When we asked him if he was okay, he told us he was fine and then smiled . . . his teeth were blue! My sister and I started laughing hysterically! It was obvious now what had happened. He was chewing on a pen and it had exploded in his mouth.

"What? What?" he screamed at us.

We were both laughing too hard to answer him, but the noise alerted our parents and they were rushing him to the bathroom in no time. Sadly he did not make it to get the turtle autographs, but he was able to rinse most of the ink out of his mouth.

When we were not standing in line to meet the stars, we were going to shows and riding the rides. I was a little nervous to go on some of the big rides. Maryellen didn't usually go on roller coasters, so if it was too scary I could always wait with her, but I didn't want to seem like a wussy. So most of the time I forced myself into line despite my trepidation. Usually I ended up enjoying myself. I just needed to get over the anticipation and fear on the way to the front of the line. One time in particular the line to the ride ended up being ten times worse than the ride itself. It was Space Mountain. At the beginning of the line, there is a video screen that shows you footage of other people's experiences on the ride. I was terrified. After some coaxing, they all (except Maryellen) convinced me to go on the ride with them. As we moved through the line, I could feel the fear rising up inside me. Every few steps there was another video screen and each one seemed to be more terrifying than the last. When I could not hold it in any longer, I started to cry.

"I don't wanna go anymore," I said loudly to anyone within earshot.

"Too late now," my brother snarked.

He was right. Just as John leaned down to comfort me we were being directed to board. I took a big gulp and climbed into the seat behind my brother. As the ride started, I covered my face and cried. Clutching the bars, I refused to open my eyes. After a while, my brother was able to talk me into opening my eyes, and he even got me to put my arms in the air and enjoy myself.

"See, it was fun wasn't it?" he said to me as we exited the ride.

"Yeah, I wanna go again!" I exclaimed.

And we did go again and again and again!

The whole trip was a dream come true. Never in a million years did I ever think I would be able to go to Disney World.

Summer Fun

During the summer my brother and sister and I stayed at the house during the day while my godparents were at work. My newfound siblings were pretty much old enough to stay at home by themselves and look after me as well, but we still had someone check in on us every now and then. On rainy days, we played hide and seek, which was my favorite because I was able to squeeze myself into the smallest of places and it took them forever to find me! The person looking had to open every cabinet and door in the house. One time I hid in the laundry hamper and ended up having to surrender when I grew tired of waiting for them to find me.

Some days the neighbor kids would come over and we would all play kickball in the backyard, or put the hose on a tarp from the garage and use it as a slip-and-slide. At night we would play "ghost in the graveyard"—basically a night version of tag with flashlights. We were always up to something.

My brother and I decided to go exploring around the property one afternoon and found a storm cellar off the creek alongside the house. My godmother later explained to me that this was where the food was kept before the time of refrigerators and ice boxes. Years ago the water did not rise as high as it does now. The tiny waterway kept the ground just cool enough to keep their food from spoiling.

This story inspired us, so that summer—before I was to move away—my siblings and I created an imaginary land within the large pine forest behind the house, where we would forage off the land and fight off mystical creatures and villains. We crafted forts and fake booby traps for our make-believe enemies, tied ropes to the trees for swinging across the water to elude our encroaching foes, and we even camped out one night in the yard and pretended it was part of one of our many missions to save our land.

Now don't get me wrong, though, it was not always fun and games. We were siblings, so we had our fair share of fights as well. My sister's favorite story to tell is that of her thirteenth birthday party. We shared a room together and she grew tired of the endless amount of stuffed animals that had taken over the room. She begged me to put them up somewhere or consolidate them to one corner of the room before her party started and I had refused. Thinking I had managed to win that fight, I was appalled to go to our room later to find that she and her friends had taken all of my stuffed animals and stuck them to the ceiling with maxi pads! I threw a fit of course and she ended up getting grounded, but it's hilarious to think about now.

Then there were the many stories they told me about our house that made my skin crawl. As if our basement was not creepy enough in itself, my sister told me that before our parents bought the house the previous owners used to lock children in the basement and burn them in the cement fireplace under our living room to heat the house. To this day I chuckle about it each time I walk down in the basement. My brother countered her story with a similar tale about our attic. Again, as if the attic was not creepy enough in itself, my brother told me that the large bags hanging from the rafters of the ceiling were old body bags that belonged to the previous owners and had been used to store the bodies of the children before they were burned. I never entered the attic by myself after hearing that one!

Vacation!

In August, my godparents took us to Nags Head, North Carolina. They rented a house on the beach and invited our family friends to join us. My godfather towed our boat behind the truck and it seemed like forever until we arrived. The beach was right outside of our front door, so we were able to spend every waking moment soaking up the sun. My sister and I walked the sand looking for shells and we all practiced surfing the waves on our boogie boards. When the weather permitted, we took the boat out on the ocean and fished. My godmother taught me to bait my hook with a live minnow and I ended up catching a sand shark! We used all different kinds of baits, depending on what we were fishing for. This was nothing like fishing in the stream by John's parent's house. (Which was where I had caught my first fish!) There we used worms for bait, and although I was good at putting them on the hook, I did not have the same confidence in removing the freshly caught fish. Luckily, my brother was close by. He heard my screams and came running to find my pole on the ground next to a flailing trout still on the line. After composing himself from hysterical laughter, he dutifully removed the fish and calmed me down. It was a bonding moment.

Our fishing excursions in Nags Head were a bit less chaotic than those at the trout stream, but they were just as fun. My brother and sister would climb onto the front of the boat to help John navigate through the random rocks and floating debris in our path as Maryellen and I sat in the back of the boat and fished. We spent the whole day on the ocean; it was incredible!

Change of Plans

I had known from the beginning of my stay with Maryellen and John that eventually I would have to leave. The following September, just a few days after my birthday, my godparents and I attended a custody hearing. My mother was up for a transfer to another correctional facility closer to where she was to be released: Illinois. She was to be released into the custody of her adoptive parents with a limited-ability ankle bracelet. Since me living with my godparents had been a temporary arrangement, this new plan created the need for the subject to be revisited. Just a few days after my birthday, we were told by a judge that because my mother was deemed unfit, I was now considered to be a ward of the state. It was declared that my mother's adoptive parents would be my legal guardians. This meant that upon my mother's release, I would need to leave my beloved godparents' home and go live with two people I barely knew. I was terrified.

The time leading up to my departure was somber. My mother was released several months after the hearing, but everyone agreed I shouldn't be pulled out of school once again, so they agreed that June would be a good time for the transfer. My godparents had a large party for me the day I was to leave and gave me a gold heart-shaped charm necklace inscribed with a loving message and their phone number, in case I ever needed them. Everyone we knew was there to say goodbye. I felt so special.

My grandparents drove straight from Illinois to Pennsylvania the night before and arrived that afternoon in a beat-up rusty pickup truck with a covered cab in matching mustard-colored paint. They stayed for several hours and mingled with people at the party. When it was time to say goodbye, I couldn't find my godfather. I started to panic until my godmother told me he was upstairs waiting for me. I guess he didn't want to say goodbye in front of everyone. I walked upstairs to find him sitting in his recliner in the bedroom. He had been crying. Rarely had I ever seen him cry, and at this moment it was my signal that it was okay to do the same. I had been holding it in throughout my farewells, but right then all I wanted to do was curl up in his lap and let the flood gates open. So I did. I clung to him as if I would never let go. After several minutes of mutual sobbing, my godmother entered the room.

In that moment, while I sat there with the two people I now considered to be my parents, I wasn't sure how to feel. I should feel happy to be reunited with my real mother, so why was I so incredibly sad? Much as I had with my godfather, I leaped from his lap and threw my arms around my godmother's waist, clinging to her for dear life. Eventually composing ourselves, I gave my godfather one last hug and walked downstairs with my godmother.

Chapter 6

My New Life

The two people hurt most by my mother's excursions were her adoptive parents. They loved her like their own, gave her everything any little girl would have dreamed of, but somehow it was never enough. Growing up, my mother always got her way. If one of her parents disagreed with her, she would pit one against the other until they were both fighting and she eventually came out on top. My grandfather was usually the one who caved first. She was "daddy's little girl" and no matter how badly she behaved, he would end up on her side. Needless to say this caused a great deal of problems in my grandparents' relationship and created additional obstacles for me as a result.

They blamed themselves for the way she was. My grandparents were convinced that if they had only ruled with a heavier hand, my mother would have turned out much differently. So, for me growing up in the Scotts' residence was beyond difficult. They believed that their daughter's dysfunction was the result of something they had done, but had no clue what that was. Raising me—their second chance—they vowed to do things differently, and they did.

My grandfather ran a tight ship; nothing went unnoticed. Any privileges my mother had been given were taken away from me. This was not something I was used to. My mother allowed me to be very independent, the more able I was to entertain myself the easier it was for her to be inconspicuous. At my godparents' house, I was not allowed to do "whatever I wanted" so to speak, but the dynamic was certainly different in regards to one's freedom and independence. From the moment I arrived at my new home, I knew that my life there was going to be a challenge. I would be living with two people I hardly knew, in a place I didn't remember, and I was scared. When we pulled into the driveway of the unfamiliar house, I remember looking at both of my grandparents as if to say: *What do I do now?* They kept talking to me as if they had known me my whole life and it left me without a response. After all, what do you say to an almost-stranger who knows everything about you?

In the time I had spent with my mother previously, I had been a growing sponge soaking up all I could. My mother had molded me into an unknowing accomplice in her moneymaking charades. Whatever she told me, I believed to be true. Why would your mother lie to you? She would have no reason to, right? I had confronted my mother about why she had lied about her name and who she really was. She told me that she had to change her identity to protect us from someone in her past. She told me she had planned to tell me the truth when I was old enough to understand and I believed her.

By the time my grandparents took over my legal guardianship, my head was full of preconceived notions of what they were like. I visited them when I was little, but I had no real recollection of that time. All I knew was what my mother told me. And what she told me were horror stories. Before leaving Pennsylvania, I was told my grandparents would try to break us apart and take me away from her. I wasn't supposed to tell them anything about our past and was enlisted to do favors for my mother without them knowing to prevent them from splitting us up.

As a result, when my grandparents came to pick me up from Maryellen and John's house that June, I didn't want to leave and I didn't understand why I had to.

The Ice Cream Shop

My mother was released into the custody of my grandparents several months before they came to pick me up from Pennsylvania. She was made to wear an ankle monitoring system that allowed her limited mobility around town. It just so happened that there was an ice cream shop on the corner by my grandparents' house that was for lease. My mother pleaded with my grandfather to cosign the agreement for her. She promised that she was ready to change and start her life fresh! This would be the perfect new beginning for her and the location was within walking distance so he would be able to check in on her whenever he wanted to. He wanted to believe her and had always had a difficult time saying no to her anyway, so he agreed. He bought "Sugar Babies" for twelve thousand dollars with the hope that mom would truly clean up her act and start a new life for the two of us.

The shop was opened in May and was in full force by the time I arrived in June. My mother even adopted a mascot! She was still living with my grandparents, and since they would not allow her to have any pets, she decided to adopt a dog and keep it at the shop. She built a dog house behind the building and fenced in the area around it. Then, she went out and adopted a mutt of a puppy at the local pound and named him after the shop: Sugar Baby.

Sugar Babies was separated into two sections. There was one door leading to the ice cream parlor and another that entered into the restaurant area. In the restaurant my mother had installed video game consoles and a jukebox that she always had playing music. She had stocked it with all of her favorite country and pop music, which she would sing along to when there were no customers.

I thought it was perfect! I could walk up to the corner anytime and get free ice cream! Plus, how cool would it be to tell friends at my new school that my mother owned and ran the local ice cream parlor? It's always hard starting at a new school, and even though I had been through the process several times, it was still a bit unnerving. At least I would have the rest of the summer to get used to the idea and grow accustomed to my new home. That September, I would be entering the fifth grade, which would be my last year in elementary school. Next year (that is if we were still living here) I would be in middle school. It would be a new school again, but everyone I meet this year would be transferring, too, so I wouldn't be alone in the process.

My grandmother and her sisters would stop in for lunch after a long day of searching for treasures at various garage sales, and my mother would allow me to fill their coffee and deliver their food. She also let me keep the tips from any of the tables I helped clear. I guess you could say it was my first paying job!

Our New Home

With Sugar Babies up and running, and my mother finally off house arrest, she decided it was time for us to move out of her parent's house and into a place of our own. She had instructed me to keep the search for our new home a secret from my grandparents until she was ready to tell them. She explained to me that they wanted to take me away from her, and that if they found out we were trying to leave they might kick her out of the house and separate us forever. Seeing as I had just met these people and my mother had kept contact with them to a minimum for my whole life, it didn't seem unreasonable to me that they could not be trusted.

We ended up finding an extremely small one bedroom house a few blocks away from the shop. It was barely enough room for the both of us, but my mother explained that I could sleep in the large closet in the living room if I wanted to. It didn't really matter to me. We usually slept in the same room anyway, and there was always the couch in the living room if I needed some space.

The interior of the house had wall-to-wall wood paneling with dark brown shag carpeting in the living room and bedroom. Just to the right, after you walked through the front door, stood a small but sunny yellow kitchen. The upper part of the walls were lined with wooden cabinets, except for one small area where a window was placed perfectly above an old cast iron sink, overlooking the front yard. The flooring resembled that of a commercial warehouse and extended to a barely functional bathroom in the very back of the kitchen. There was a small shower stall in the corner and the toilet was pushed right up to the sink so you could rest your arm on it if you needed to. The house was set back on a fairly large lot with a gigantic climbing tree to the right of the front door. I fell in love with the place almost immediately! My mother must have as well, because she signed the lease that same day. Now we just had to break the news to my grandparents . . .

My Mother's New Girlfriend

My mother started setting up the cottage before my grandparents had any idea that we were planning to move out. As soon as our new home was ready for us to move into, she sat down with her parents and told them that she had found a place to live and wanted to take me with her. I remember listening to them argue about whether I should be able to go with her or not, and I could not understand why they were so adamant about keeping us separated. The place was less than five minutes from where they lived and the ice cream parlor was located right in between. It was perfect!

After some arguing, they compromised and decided that I would be able to spend time at the new house, but would still need to sleep at theirs. Any overnight visits with my mother would need to be agreed upon by both parties and scheduled in advance. The next day, my mother moved out.

My mother told me later that she agreed to this because she knew it was the only way they would let her leave, and that once some time had passed they would back down.

I was still able to see my mom every day. She came over in the mornings to take me to school and would pick me up if she was not working. After a while, I was able to spend the weekends at the cottage with her and even started to bring some of my things over to her place and leave them there.

In our time together, my mother began telling me about a woman she had become very close to while she was serving her last sentence. Her name was Jeannette, but my mom called her "J.J." She explained that they had stayed in touch and that she wanted this woman to come live with us the following month when she was done serving her time. I didn't have much choice in the matter and I knew that, so I chose not to voice any objection to the idea. By this point I was used to sharing my mother's time with other people. On the surface, she was a very likable person. People seemed to be drawn to her free spirit and fun-loving attitude. Again, I was not to say anything to my grandparents because, according to her, they would overreact and stop letting me stay with her.

The day J.J. was released, she and my mother picked me up from school and drove straight to my grandparents' house. My mother told me to stay in the car. She said she needed to talk to them alone. She went inside the house while J.J. and I sat in the car and waited for what seemed like forever. J.J. and I hit it off almost immediately. She reminded me of my mother in a lot of ways and I felt very comfortable with her. She also seemed to really care for my mother and that was the most important to me, so as far as I was concerned she was in!

After a while, my mother came storming out of the house with my grandfather behind her yelling to her to come back inside. Before he made it to the end of the driveway we were already down the road. My mother was crying hysterically and I could not understand a word she was saying. J.J. kept trying to console her, but it was no use.

By the time we arrived at the cottage, she had stopped sobbing and turned silent. Without a word, we all got out of the car and walked inside. My mother and J.J. sat in the living room talking about the fight and I pretended not to listen to them as I sat in the bedroom playing video games. I overheard something about my grandfather being upset with her because of her relationship with J.J., and I assumed it was because she had also been incarcerated. Maybe he thought she would be a bad influence on my mom or something. Eventually, I grew tired of trying to figure it all out and tuned them both out.

When they were done talking, my mother started dinner. After we were finished eating, J.J. suggested we all watch a movie together before bed. I thought that was a great idea and picked out one of my favorites. We all curled up on my mom's bed in front of the television and I must have dozed off, because I remember waking up as the movie was ending. My eyes were still closed and I noticed that my mother was no longer lying right next to me as she had been before. Before I could turn to look, I heard my mother ask, "Should we move her to the living room?"

"No, she might wake up . . . Let's just be quiet," J.J. replied in a soft voice.

I wasn't sure what was going on . . . until I heard them kissing. My body froze as the feeling of fear took over. I didn't know what to do. I wanted to run screaming from the room, but I was scared that I might get in trouble for doing so. I decided that I would have to pretend to have just awoken and maybe they would notice and stop. Just as I prepared to stretch out my arm as if to yawn myself awake, I heard my mother moan, followed by some strange vocals from J.J. I immediately jumped up from the bed and, with my back still to them, I walked out of the room. As I was leaving, I heard my mother ask, "Should I go check on her?"

"She is probably still half asleep, I'm sure she is fine," replied J.J. in a dismissive voice.

I was barely out of the room before I heard them pick up right where they had left off. I tried drowning them out by putting a pillow over my head, and even went and sat in the bathroom for a while, but it was no use. I didn't sleep the rest of the night. My mind was racing. I understood now what they had meant earlier about my grandfather being upset about their "relationship." I didn't care that they were dating; I actually thought it was kind of cool. Secretly, I never wanted my mother to start dating again after her and Kerry separated. No one would be able to take his place and I didn't want anyone to try. I had never entertained the idea of my mother dating a woman and it was calming to me to put aside the worry of someone trying to step in as my father. I liked J.J., and if she was in a relationship with my mother it wouldn't really be like she was trying to replace anyone so I didn't see the harm in it.

However, much like the disgust anyone would feel hearing their parents' intimate relations, I too would have preferred not to have been a part of their most recent reunion. If we would all be living together, that would definitely be something my mother and I needed to discuss. I decided to talk to her about it the next time we were alone. It was an awkward conversation to have with anyone, especially your mother, and I thought it best that we speak in private.

The next night, I stayed at my grandparents' house. They drilled me with questions about my mother's new "friend" and I pretended to be oblivious. After the night before, I had no desire to delve into the subject any further. At least for now.

A few nights later, I was at the cottage with my mother and J.J., and my grandfather came over. He started banging on the door and screaming that she wasn't supposed to have me tonight, especially with her girlfriend there! He had somehow found out that J.J. was HIV positive and used to be addicted to crack cocaine. My mother refused to answer the door at first, but fearing he would call the police, she told me to hide in the bathroom with J.J. and she let him inside. They screamed at each other in the living room for several minutes. I had my head buried in J.J.'s lap and had been crying too excessively to pay any attention to what was being said. Then, I heard the front door slam and, shortly after, the bathroom door was flung open to reveal my similarly distraught mother. She said it would be better if I just stayed with them tonight and took me to their house immediately.

Let's Go!

The next day my mother and J.J. showed up at school with the car packed to the brim with our belongings, and pulled me out of class. I had been through this before. I knew exactly what was about to happen. I pleaded with my mother not to do this, but she told me she had no other choice and if I wanted to be with her then I would have to come with them right then. The decision was obvious to me. I shrugged at my mother, turned toward the car, opened the door, and climbed in. My mother followed suit and we pulled away from the school in silence.

I barely said a word the whole trip, but that didn't keep my mother and J.J. from talking at me. My mother justified her behavior by saying that my grandfather had accused her of stealing from the restaurant and threatened to put her back in jail. This was their way of splitting us up, so she had to take me as far away from them as possible and we would have to change our names again. I frowned at the notion and J.J. piped in about how fun it would be to choose whatever names we wanted. I wasn't impressed.

The plan was to drive down to Florida to live with J.J.'s mother until we were able to find our own place. We drove straight through until we hit the Florida border. Once we crossed over, we stopped off at a small motel alongside the road. It was old and dingy, but regardless of its condition, I fell asleep as soon as my head hit the pillow.

After what I assumed to have been several hours, I was awoken by someone coughing and several voices that I did not recognize. With my eyes still closed, I slowly rolled over, pulling the covers up over my head with a yawn. I was now able to peek through the covers unnoticed to take in my surroundings. All the people in the room were behind me now and seemed to be undisturbed by my movement. I could hear my mother talking to a strange man about smoking. He seemed to be reassuring her about it for some reason.

I opened my eyes to see the bathroom door directly in front of me. I wanted more than anything to remove myself from this situation. I wasn't sure what was going on, but I knew there were a lot of people there that I did not know and it freaked me out. If I could manage to get to the bathroom and lock the door behind me, I knew I would feel better somehow. Without another thought I snuck out of the covers and ran into the bathroom, catching a glimpse of white powder on the dresser as I slammed the door! I immediately locked the door behind me and crouched down beside it. Several minutes passed and I was beginning to feel a bit less overwhelmed until my mother began knocking on the door loudly and shaking the handle. She pleaded with me to open the door over and over again, but I just sat there staring in front of me without a word. I knew I would have to open the door at some point, but I decided to wait until I was ready.

When I finally decided to give in to her pleas, she came running at me, slamming the door behind her. She knelt down in front of me and I could tell she was looking at me, but her eyes were almost black and it was as if she was looking right past me. Beads of sweat rolled down her face.

"What did I tell you?" she asked and then answered herself with, "stay under the covers and be quiet when you wake up."

"Please stop," I muttered to her. Referring to what I now knew was happening in the other room. I wasn't the sharpest kid, but I had been around long enough to know that the white powder I had seen on the dresser was connected to the cooking and smoking conversation I had overheard before running to the bathroom.

"I will, I promise, but you need to go to bed . . . I won't do it after tonight, I promise." She nodded as to confirm my acceptance of her offer and I just turned, opened the bathroom door, walked directly to the bed, lifted the covers, and climbed underneath. I pulled the blanket over my head, leaving a tiny hole through which I could see the television set playing some random distraction. I tuned in slowly and intently as I gradually faded into the freedom of sleep.

Chapter 7

Florida

A fter leaving the hotel, we stayed at J.J.'s mother's house somewhere in Florida. Her mother lived in a small two bedroom house in a busy neighborhood. My mother and J.J. shared a room and I slept on the couch. My mother had packed what she felt was needed, so we didn't have much. She made sure I had my favorite stuffed animals and dolls to keep me content. J.J.'s mother was extremely nice and I was warming up to the idea of starting over again. From what my mother had told me, we really had no other choice, and she promised that everything would work out perfectly once we were able to get our new birth certificates. We made plans to dye our hair and she told me that she would even allow me to cut my hair if I wanted to. This was huge, because my mother always insisted on me having extremely long hair. I had begged her to let me cut it short, but she always refused. I was very excited at this new change of heart! She told me that I wouldn't be able to start school until our new identities were in place and I had no objections to that.

Behind the house there was a small yard with a clothesline where I helped my mother and J.J. hang the laundry. We had only been there for about a week when one afternoon we were all outside doing just that, and J.J.'s mother came running out to tell us that the police were there for my mother. I threw my arms around Mom and began to cry. She pulled me off and kneeled down in front of me.

"It's okay," she said, looking directly into my eyes.

I just blubbered back at her. As she pulled me in close, hugging me tighter than usual, she whispered, "You have to let them take me. Go to J.J."

I followed my mother's orders and walked over to stand by J.J.

Police officers flooded the backyard as my mother, still kneeling, raised her hands above her head. One of the officers came up behind her, pulled her hands down behind her back, and secured the cuffs. As they walked my mother to the cop car, I turned to J.J. and held on to her with all my might. I was crying hysterically. I had no idea what was going to happen next, but at least I was with someone I knew and would be able to stay with her until my mother was released. Or so I thought.

Still clutching onto J.J., I felt someone tap on my shoulder. I turned around to find two police officers looking at me with very long faces.

"You need to come with us now, honey," one of them said in a somber voice.

I screamed in dismay and turned back to clutch onto J.J. She asked the officer if we could have a moment and, resting her head on mine, she reassured me as much as she could and told me that I needed to be strong. I felt another tap on my shoulder and this time I turned around to find J.J.'s mother holding one of my favorite stuffed animals. As I took it into my arms, I looked up to the officer who had addressed me before and he nodded back to me as if to relay his understanding that I was agreeing to comply. I gave J.J. and her mother each one last hug and turned to the officer, who was now extending his hand to me. I grasped it tightly and we walked through the house together. As we exited the front door I could see the large line of police vehicles parked along the street. Their lights were still flashing, but their sirens were off. Walking up to his vehicle, I could see my mother sitting in the police car behind his. She watched intently as the police officer opened his door and motioned me inside. Not knowing when I would see her again, I took one last long look before I turned away and stepped inside.

The Flight

As I sat in the police station waiting to find out what would happen next, I began to think about all of the things my mother had told me about why we had left Illinois. I was certain that this was all my grandparents' fault and I hoped I would be sent back to my godparents instead of them. The officers in the station tried to make me as comfortable as possible, but I barely said a word to any of them. Eventually a social worker came in to tell me where I would be going. The social worker explained that my mother was going to be transported back to Illinois and that I would be put on the first available flight back there as well. I knew this meant that I would be going to be my grandparents' house, so I didn't bother asking. Shortly after our conversation, I was driven to the airport and put on a flight home, just as she had said.

When we arrived, a flight attendant walked me through the airport to where my grandparents were both waiting to pick me up. As they reached out to embrace me, I pulled away and told them I hated them. I was convinced they had ruined everything, and I really didn't want to be there. Unaware of the tales my mother had told me, they were completely clueless as to why I was behaving this way; they were crushed.

Just as the social worker had explained, my mother was expedited back to Illinois and charged with child abduction and three counts of grand theft, including one for grand theft auto for stealing the "getaway" car! My grandparents later dropped the abduction charges and she was sentenced to five years of probation after serving just a few months. I was able to visit her monthly up until that time. No contact visits; glass and phone only.

Time Served

After my mother served her sentence for the grand theft charges, she was once again released into the custody of my grandparents. By this time I was starting at a new middle school. I was in sixth grade.

I had kept my mother's history quiet from most of my friends, except for my best friend at the time: Gabby. Gabby and I had been friends since fifth grade, so she knew what had happened the year before in Florida and she never let it affect our friendship. I told everyone else at school that my mother surprised me with a vacation to Florida and we didn't call anyone because we were having so much fun! Gabby knew the truth, though. Her parents knew my story as well and they never treated me any different, either. For most of that year and the next, Gabby and I were inseparable!

Before my mother was released, I had talked my grandparents into letting me take tumbling classes with Gabby as an after-school activity. I couldn't wait to show off everything I had learned to my mother. She was again put on a limited-mobility ankle bracelet as part of her probation, but her parole officer agreed to allow her to take me to my classes.

All was fine until one day when my mother left during my class to run to the gas station and was pulled over for speeding. When the officer ran her license he found an outstanding warrant for violating her probation the year before and arrested her on the spot. At the end of class, I noticed that my grandfather was there waiting for me. I felt all eyes looking in my direction as I asked him where my mother was and he told me we would talk about it at home. As it turned out, the warrant was no longer active, but had not been updated in the system for some reason. My mother was released and the charges cleared, but it didn't matter to Gabby's mom. After that night, Gabby was no longer able to come over to my house. Her mother would allow me to come over to their house, but I guess she just didn't feel safe with Gabby being around my mother. Over the next few years, Gabby and I ended up drifting apart. By the time we reached high school, we barely spoke to each other.

Chapter 8

Moving On

After a while, my mother got a job working at an animal shelter and eventually she was able to have the ankle bracelet removed. She still had to attend regular meetings with her probation officer, but she had a great deal more freedom. This began to cause problems between her and my grandparents because she was using their car and was never completely honest about where she was going. I tried not to get in the middle of the arguments, but that was impossible. There were many, many times where I ended up at the center of my grandparents' interrogations. By this time I was pretty skilled at knowing what I should and should not tell them. For example, I was not to tell them about our visits to see her biological siblings. As she explained to me, my grandparents did not want her to associate with them because they were afraid she would find out the truth about her adoption. She was convinced that my grandparents had somehow stolen her from her biological family and they had been covering it up for years.

If this were truly the case, I could see why they would be worried. My mother and I were spending a lot of time with her biological family and I loved it. My mother was one of six children. She had four sisters and a brother. Everyone lived close by except for one of her sisters who lived in Minnesota with her husband and two children. Her biological mother, Mary, had passed away a few years earlier and her biological father, Robert, had moved out of state, so we were not able to visit with them. This was unfortunate, considering I had very few memories of them, but the times I was able to recall were always pleasant. My biological grandmother played dolls with me as a child and I remember her as a very loving, gentle woman. She was just under five feet tall, very petite, with long dark hair that she always kept pulled back in a French twist. She and my biological grandfather lived in a trailer park community just outside of town. The youngest of my mother's siblings—her brother, Bobby—lived with them up until my grandmother's passing. I remembered playing Nintendo with him during the day and spending time playing computer games in my grandfather's office at night. He always kept a jar of walnuts next to the computer that I would devour during game play.

After some time of hanging with our biological family, my mother was introduced to her sister's husband's brother, Terry, and they began dating. He was extremely nice! He had been married once before and still lived in the house he and his wife had purchased before they were married. He seemed to fall for my mother immediately. They began spending a lot of time together and most of the time I would stay home but, after a while, they began inviting me to join them on their movie and dinner dates. She introduced him to her adoptive parents and they seemed to be accepting of him. In what seemed like only a few months, my mother and I were moving in with him, and several months later they were getting married. I was indifferent to the idea. I wasn't very happy where I was currently, so it didn't really seem to matter that I was leaving to live in another strange place. I wouldn't be changing schools or anything so it really made no difference to me where we were.

Terry was overly accepting of me and, to be honest, I was kind of rotten. I knew he had to be nice to me because he wanted to make my mother happy, so I had a hard time believing that he actually cared. I know now that I was very wrong and I wish I would have been easier on him. Before I moved in, he completely redid the room that would be my bedroom. He let me pick out the paint, carpet, and all new furniture. I decided on a bright magenta color for the carpet and the walls had a slight pink hue to them. I picked out a white bunk bed with a desk on one side. He surprised me one day with a white television to match my bed and a new black TV stand complete with shelving for my VCR and video game console. Not only was this the first time in years that I had my own bedroom, but I had never owned anything as nice as the furniture in that room—let alone had my own television set! I refused to admit it then, but I was really impressed.

My bedroom was not the only room that changed when we moved into Terry's house. My mother had somewhat of an obsession with cows and decided to make it the theme for our kitchen. She lined everything she could with cow contact paper, from the inside of the cabinets to the outlet covers and switch plates. She even went as far as to purchase and install a wall phone with the cow spot pattern. Terry had an extreme man cave in the basement where he crafted her custom shelves for her collectible cow figurines that she purchased in bulk from online catalogs.

When she was finished with the kitchen, she moved on to the living room. Her theme for the living room was bunnies. She covered the backs of our living room armchairs, couch, and loveseat with bunny throw blankets and purchased small chairs on which to seat her many stuffed rabbits. Every surface contained something bunny-related and the walls were lined with more custom crafted shelves for her many collectible figurines (bunny-related, of course).

Their bedroom was not as obnoxious, but it still had a theme of its own: cats. Just outside their bedroom was a completely different story. My mother used the wall alongside the steps to showcase what we jokingly referred to as her "shrine" to her favorite country music star: Reba McEntire. My mother purchased every single item available through the fan club and, together with calendar and magazine photos, created a collage of memorabilia that filled the entire space. It was a bit overwhelming, but it was tastefully done.

Thanks to my mother, I met Reba McEntire once in one of the most embarrassing moments of my life. I was a huge fan (still am), so I was thrilled when my mother told me we not only had tickets to one of her concerts, but we had VIP access as well! Which meant that after the concert we would be able to attend the invite-only meet-and-greet session with Reba. It took place in the upper half of the arena. We wouldn't actually get to meet her—it was more of a question and answer session—but it was still pretty cool!

The concert was amazing. I had never seen a performance like it. My mother and I were front row center, so we didn't miss a minute of the show! When the concert ended my mother rushed to the VIP area. I needed to use the bathroom and there was one right next to the door, so my mother agreed to meet me inside. I finished my business, took a deep breath, and opened the door to the meeting room. The room was separated into two sections of chairs aligned into rows, and pretty much every seat was filled. Directly in front of me was a long aisle and at the end of that aisle stood the country legend herself! I scanned the room for my mother and before I made it to the right side of the room, I heard Reba say, "Hello there ma'am, did you lose something?" Before turning my head, I closed my eyes for a moment and prayed she was not talking to who I thought she might be. Just as I opened my eyes, I heard my mother reply, "My daughter!" I turned to see her. She was the only one in the entire room standing and looking around. As she saw me, she exclaimed, "There she is!" as she pointed in my direction. Every person in the room turned and looked at me! I am not sure what shade of red my face was at that point, but I'm sure it was slowly approaching a bright rosy color. I looked at my mother through wide eyes, and then turned my gaze toward Reba. She smiled and returned my look with a gaze of understanding. Not saying a word, I walked toward my mother and sat down. I was mortified, but at least I can say I have met one of my idols!

By the end of that summer, I was all settled in at Terry's, but I would still spend the night at my grandparents' house from time to time because I was able to walk to school from their house. If I stayed at Terry's, we would have to get up much earlier because he lived about an hour from my middle school. Without my mother living there, the divide between my grandparents and myself was becoming nonexistent. They seemed to be less inquisitive about my mother and more interested in how I was doing. After a while, I once again looked forward to spending time with them.

My Best Friend

On the first day of eighth grade, I met someone who would change my life forever. For me, the first day of school had always been a bit nerve-racking. I never looked forward to navigating the halls looking for new classrooms and being forced to meet more new people. Even now the idea of entering a room filled with strangers and having to take a seat makes my skin crawl. It's not the social aspect of it, but rather the nervousness related to being the center of attention in a room full of your peers. On this particular day, I was feeling just that way as I walked in to my U.S. Government class and realized there was not a single person in the class that I knew. I scanned the room for possible seating and noticed an open desk next to a slender, wide-eyed girl who was making eye contact with me from across the room. I moved toward her and said in a nervous voice, "I don't know anyone in here, can I sit by you?"

Without hesitation, she nodded in agreement and I comfortably took my seat. We have been best friends ever since!

Amanda lived with her stepfather just a few blocks from my grandparents' house. Which was perfect, because we were able to walk to each other's houses pretty much whenever we wanted. There was a park directly between both places, so we spent a lot of our time there, too. As it turned out, we were in a few other classes together as well, and after a while we were a force to be reckoned with. One of the people who felt our wrath was the new science teacher that also taught our homeroom class. During sixth and seventh grade, science was taught by a teacher who was by far every student's favorite. He was one of those teachers that seemed to be able to relate to everyone in one way or another. He had a passion for teaching and it showed. We all loved him. These were big shoes to fill for someone new. And as if that wasn't enough of a challenge, this new teacher had to teach a bunch of students on the verge of entering high school—talk about cocky! We did everything from pretending to pass notes and eating candy in class to refusing to obey the hall pass policies. Anything we could make more difficult, we did. One time we each used a blank piece of notebook paper underneath a test to pretend that we were cheating. When he confronted us, we acted outraged by his accusations and held up the empty pages with smirks on our faces. Amanda and I were not the only ones; another group of people in our class wrote him a series of long anonymous love letters, which they left on his desk each day for a week. Boy kids can be mean! In our defense, Amanda and I did end up visiting him after we graduated to apologize for our rude behavior if that counts for anything. He seemed appreciative of the gesture.

Halloween 1995

That Halloween my mother and I planned a sleepover party with a few of my girlfriends. She would pick us all up after school and we would go back to the house, which would be decorated in the spookiest of fashions. Along with the festive decorations, the night before the party, my mother made a cake and decorated it to resemble a graveyard. She used tea biscuits for the tombstones and covered the "ground" with candy pumpkins, marshmallow ghosts, and gummy worms. I helped her put cobwebs on all of the windows, placing random spiders throughout. It was Halloween everywhere! She had also purchased a large package of toilet paper from the local supermarket and told me that if no one told their parents that she would let us all go "TP" the neighborhood. My mom was awesome!

And as my mother always does, she took it too far. At the end of the day, my sleepover buddies and I made our way out of school to where my mother was to pick us up. We were no sooner out of the building when I saw her. My mother had painted her entire body green and dressed herself as the Wicked Witch of the West—complete with a wart-covered nose and a broom—and she was standing in the middle of the schoolyard for everyone to see. I was mortified!

I rushed her to the car and out of sight as fast as I could. My friends reassured me later that it was actually pretty cool and that I shouldn't worry about it, but I was fairly certain they were just trying to make me feel better. Regardless, the rest of the night was a hit. We watched movies, ate junk food, and toilet-papered the neighborhood (shhh). I had received three brand-new girly games for my birthday: Girl Talk, Dream Phone, and Mall Madness. We played every one of them until we passed out around three A.M..

Much to my surprise, the following week at school no one even mentioned my mother's costume, and I was truly thankful for that.

Our New Puppy!

That November my mother decided that we needed to get a dog and convinced Terry to let us do so. From the beginning, she was dead set on adopting a sheltie-type breed and once Terry gave her the go-ahead she called all of the shelters in town asking that they call her if a sheltie, collie, or similar breed came in. A week or two passed, and then we received a call from one of the shelters stating that they had just picked up two puppies. They were possible sheltie mixes that had been abandoned along one of the main roads in town. After school that day my mother and I went down to the shelter to see them.

The two of them were brother and sister. Neither had been bathed yet and they were just filthy. Their long hair was matted in clumps and you could barely see their eyes. My heart went out to both of these poor puppies. I wanted to take both of them home. If they were siblings, I thought it would be horrible to split them up and I pleaded with my mother to consider the idea. She stood firm on choosing just one, but once I had voiced my opinion, she told the woman running the shelter to please let us know if the other puppy was not adopted. This was reassuring.

I chose the boy puppy, with his long snout and his scruffy little body. After careful consideration, I decided to name him Gizmo. The agreement between my mother, Terry, and I was that Gizmo would be my responsibility. I jumped at the opportunity! He slept in my room with me at night, and I would take him outside and feed him in the mornings before school. Then he would ride along to drop me off and either go back to our house with my mother or stay at my grandparents' house until I was finished with school, so I could see him right away. It was great! He was my very own companion dog.

Unwrapped

As Christmastime approached, I began to notice some tension between my mother and Terry. Over the last few months, my mother had been spending a lot of money and she wasn't really working that I knew of. During the day, she babysat for one of her biological sisters, Lynn, but I was pretty sure she wasn't making a ton of money doing that. Lynn was in her early thirties. She was the mother of five children: four girls and a boy, who was the youngest. She and her husband, James, (Terry's brother) worked at a large car manufacturing plant and sometimes they worked the same overnight shift, which made it virtually impossible to find a cost-effective child care option. Terry worked at a manufacturing plant and I knew that he made good money, so I figured that was where all the money was coming from. It wasn't my place to ask, so I didn't. It was when she started purchasing concert tickets for hundreds of dollars that I began to see it all start to unravel. We were going to big-name shows and sitting in the front row, right in the center, time after time. We saw Kenny Rogers, Vince Gill, Patty Loveless, Reba McEntire (several times), and Tracy Byrd. The Kenny Rogers concert was a Christmas celebration. He came down into the audience and walked up to each of us in the front row inviting us to sing along. For a moment, I was sharing the microphone with Kenny Rogers . . . That was awesome! As much as I enjoyed it, I knew it had to have cost a pretty penny. I began to worry that what had happened with Kerry was occurring all over again, and it frightened me. I was really happy with my life at that moment. I didn't want anything to change.

On Christmas morning, my grandparents were invited to our house for gift opening. As with every holiday with my mother, the house was over the top with decorations and our small tree in the corner of the living room was surrounded by stacks and stacks of presents. So much so that it was impossible to see the tree from some locations in the room. It took us three hours to open presents that morning. Almost every one of them from my mother to one of us. As I unwrapped each gift, my gratitude slowly began to fade and my disdain for my mother's actions began to rise. I could not help but to ask myself how she had been able to purchase all of these gifts. Most of all, I think Terry—who knew she was not working—wondered how many of those needless gifts he had actually purchased. With each tear of the wrapping paper, I could see the dollar signs accumulating in his eyes. The tension in the room thickened and even my grandparents seemed to be growing suspicious of how this had all been possible.

When we were finished, I took all my new possessions to my room and waited for the yelling between my mother and Terry to begin, but it never came. Not that night at least.

Several months later, they filed for divorce and my mother and I moved back in with her adoptive parents. I didn't mind this too much since my school was close and my best friend still lived up the street. We stayed there until we found a small house in a gated community thirty minutes or so from where my grandparents lived. There we would start all over again.

D.C. Trip

I t was a tradition at my middle school for the graduating eighth grade to plan a trip to Washington, D.C., at the end of each year. My mother was hesitant to let me go at first, but believe it or not, my grandparents talked her into letting me attend. Our chaperones were a collection of science and social studies teachers from a variety of grade levels. Each of them were assigned to a group and in charge of gathering everyone together for each of our daily excursions.

We had all picked our hotel room groups months before. There were four of us to a room: boys were on one floor and girls on another. We were a rowdy bunch and we were not the only group of eighth graders in the hotel, so the hotel staff had their hands full. As did the teaching staff. During the day, when we were not touring the city, we were allowed to spend time enjoying the facilities and mingle back and forth between floors. At the end of the day the adults came by each room to ensure there was no coed mingling and they supposedly kept an eye on us throughout the night, but I am not sure how a constant watch was really possible. For the most part we all behaved; we were just a little obnoxious.

It was a great learning experience and I forged friendships on that trip that made a lasting impact on the rest of my life. There was a group of us that palled around together back then. Amanda and myself of course, our friend Sydney whom we had both known since grade school, and our two other chums: Chris and Tim. Grunge was the style then and we all relished in it. Our walls were filled with posters and shrines to our favorite artists, and we were most often found wearing ripped-up blue jeans and baggy T-shirts.

As the summer approached, Amanda and I began testing our boundaries, as people our age often did, and ended up finding ourselves in a great deal of trouble when we were caught smoking a cigarette next to her bedroom window. Her stepfather's girlfriend called my mother and decided that we should all have a meeting. We all met a few days before our eighth grade graduation, which made for very interesting conversation with our families after the ceremony. My mother tried to be authoritative with me, but I reminded her that she was the last person to lecture me about anything. She pretty much dropped it after that.

Chapter 9

Mother's New Friends

M y mother's divorce from Terry was finalized in May of 1996; neither party appeared in court.

By this time, my mother and I were renting a house in Candlewick, a gated community in Poplar Grove, Illinois. We were miles away from town, but the community had a pool and a park to keep me occupied. After school ended, I picked up a job babysitting for the couple next door. They had two rambunctious boys that really kept me on my toes, but they were sweet and the job paid well. Mom was still not working that I knew of, but somehow she had enough money to start hanging out at the taverns with her sister almost every night. I later found out she had been stealing my babysitting money from the top drawer of my dresser and had emptied out my savings account. She was barely home. When she did make an appearance, she was usually not in the most coherent of mental states.

After a while, my mother completely stopped going grocery shopping and many times I was left home with nothing to eat, except for a cupboard full of premade brownie mix she had purchased at a wholesale store just before we moved in. I chowed down on this multiple times; spooning it directly from the box. In the event that my mother was gone for more than a few days, I would make up an excuse to go to my grandparents' or Amanda's house. I was careful not to stay away too long, though, because I still had my dog, Gizmo, and two cats to take care of if she was not there.

I was never comfortable inviting anyone over to our house in Candlewick, except for Amanda. With my mother's new friends, I just never knew what would happen and Amanda was the only one I trusted to keep the embarrassment quiet. One particular day, I arrived home to find my mother and several of her friends snorting cocaine off the kitchen counter. Luckily I was alone, so I just walked back to my room and locked the door behind me. I blasted my music and ignored them for the rest of the night, leaving my room for the sole purpose of using the bathroom. I had brought snacks home with me that day, so I was able to hole up in my bedroom until the party was over. The next morning I ventured out to find my mother passed out on her bedroom floor but, to my relief, everyone else had gone. I cleaned up the mess from the night before—in the loudest manner possible—until my barely clothed mother staggered out of her bedroom to tell me to shut up. I gave her a snotty little smirk and went back into my room.

The summer continued much like this until eventually all we did was fight with each other. She continued to spend most of every day at the bar and by sundown she was so drunk that she either never came home or called the house completely trashed and nostalgic, begging that I call someone to come get her. Then by the time we'd make it down there she'd usually have left already or had been thrown outside where she sat crying and screaming about how unloved she was and the fact that no one cared. And I thought I was dramatic!

I remember one time my mother came to pick Amanda and I up from the pool in Belvidere Park and was accompanied by one of her new friends: Janet. They were in a state that was so far from sober, it was sadly obvious. Amanda and I talk about it to this day. Thank god it was Amanda who was with me and no one else because I would have been so embarrassed (and still was a little). My mother was driving and Janet was in the front seat, overalls half latched and singing . . . badly! It seemed like the louder she sang the more my mother swerved, but thankfully we ended up making it home safely. It was serious at the time, but we laugh about it now. Whenever we hear the song Janet was wailing, we will mimic the women's sad vocal attempts in a laughing fit of reminiscence. We have so many of those memories. I am so lucky to have had Amanda in my life to experience this craziness with.

What's Up with Mom?

E ventually her excursions caught up with her and she was arrested in July for driving while intoxicated. As a result, her license was suspended and her car impounded. She was released on the same day as one of her parole officer's home visits was scheduled. At the time, I had no idea where she was, but I knew better than to tell him that. Instead, I told him that she had run to the store and must have forgot he was coming. He instructed me to tell her to call him as soon as she returned, and I did.

A few weeks later I went to visit my godparents in Pennsylvania. My mother seemed to be a bit overemotional when she took me to the airport, but it seemed to me that she was always acting odd then, so I didn't think much of it. When she hugged me goodbye, she seemed to be holding on for dear life. I finally had to pull myself away and I noticed that she was sobbing. I told her everything would be okay and that I would see her soon. Little did I know, this couldn't be further from the truth.

When I landed, I called home to let my mother know I had made it safely, and my uncle Bobby answered the phone. He and his wife had recently separated and my mother had allowed him to move in with us. He was her biological brother and in many forms he was like her twin. He was known for his pathological lying and get-rich-quick schemes that never made him rich. Regardless, we got along very well and for the remainder of my visit to Pennsylvania he was my only source of information about what was happening in my absence. Every time I called, my mother was never around. I was suspicious and I think a part of me knew that she had left again. I just didn't want to believe it. I tried to enjoy myself, but it was hard to do having no idea where my mother was or whether she would be there when I got home. I didn't want to disappoint my godparents by asking to leave early, but when the call came regarding the murder of my aunt Lynn's husband I decided it was time to leave. My uncle Bobby had made the call and informed me that he would fill me in on the gruesome details when I returned. As mentioned before, James was the father of five young children; his death was devastating.

My godparents were more than understanding and arranged to have my return date pushed up so I could be there to mourn with my family. I tried calling the house to let my mother know that I would be coming back early, but she was not there of course. Bobby answered and assured me that he would be there to pick me up and that he would pass along the information to my mother.

Again?

I landed in Rockford on a Saturday and my uncle Bobby picked me up from the airport as promised. On the way home, he told me that he hadn't seen my mom in over a week and that before she left she had been throwing parties, having sex in my bed with random folks, and doing a lot of drugs. There was a rumor floating around that she was going to be sent back to jail for violating her probation, so she ran out of town with a local biker who was a member of the Hell's Angels. I thought that sounded just like her and even though the biker portion of the story may have been an elaboration, I was sure she had fled the state.

He also told me that my grandparents had stopped over to the house one day while I was gone and found my dog, Gizmo, outside in the yard with no food or water. They took him and my cats, Buttons and Flash, to their house for safekeeping. I figured that was probably best. If she was truly gone, I had no idea what my living situation would be like.

I walked through the door to find the house somewhat the same. Most of her clothes were still there; she had only taken a few things. This shed a glimmer of hope on the situation for me; maybe there was still a chance that she would be coming home. All we could do was wait.

On the third day of waiting, the landlord came over to let us know that we were thirteen hundred dollars behind on rent. As it turns out, my mother had tried to use one of Bobby's checks to pay it, but the account had just been closed, so the check came back fraudulent. He told us we had twenty-four hours to vacate the house. I nodded to him in compliance and shut the door.

I immediately walked into my mother's room and fell to my knees.

"Are you okay?" Bobby asked as he followed me.

"Sure," I said as he kneeled down to hug me.

In this moment, I remember thinking that I should have seen the signs of her readiness to flee and somehow I should have been able to prevent it. However, I decided this was not the time to dwell on why this had happened, but instead time to focus on what I needed to do next.

After I gained my bearings, I made the necessary phone calls to my aunts and my grandparents to let them know of this new development. They all came over to help me pack up our things and vacate the house. Since my grandparents still had legal custody of me, it was only logical that I move back in with them.

It was the summer before my freshman year of high school and once again I was without my mother. I had no idea where she was. Leaving was normal for her, but she had never left me before. I worked through it in my own way; mostly by writing. I began to express myself in all forms: short stories, poetry, and aimless rants. I had saved a bottle of her favorite perfume and would spray it on my pillow at night before bed. Prior to her departure, I had hated the overindulgence that scent represented, but somehow now what had once been annoying had become comforting.

I also began writing in a diary every day, in the form of a letter to my mother. I hoped she would come home and I would be able to give it to her and tell her how I felt after she left me.

She Is Alive

We eventually received a lifeline from Mom. My uncle Bobby called and told me that she had called one of her old stomping grounds: The Saloon, and had spoken with her sister Lynn on the phone. I guess she had been looking for Terry and/or Janet. Lynn told him that when she asked mom why she had left, she said she just had to, and then she hung up. That was it.

I remember feeling relieved to know she was still breathing and hurt by the realization that she was simply choosing not to come home. To me this meant it was really happening: She had left me and she was not coming back. She left me, alone, in a house with her memories all around me. I felt myself striving to get out of her shadow, and every day trying as hard as I could to not be like her, even though I felt at times that everyone around me somehow assumed that it was inevitable! I swore to myself that even if I never do anything of note, I will never be like her. I focused each day on finding the joy and hope in life. As a child, I remember my mother telling me that if I was ever in trouble, I should just turn around and run away. That was easy for her to say; the pain of all of her mistakes has yet to catch up with her. I, however, am the one she left behind. I have never been given the choice to run away and hide from her flaming bridges. Instead, I am left to face it, deal with it, and rise above it. So, everything she has run away from I have rushed into and conquered. I am thankful, in a sense, for her horrible decisions and selfish endeavors because had I not been the result of irresponsibility during the heat of passion, I would not have become the lessons learned from her mistakes. It broke my heart to hear that she had called the bar instead of her own daughter, but it also added to the distance between us and the reality of who she really is.

Mixed Feelings

I started high school that September and I tried to remain positive. Things at home were challenging to say the least. I was still working through my feelings of abandonment from my mother, and operating under the assumption that her claims that my grandparents were evil and working against my happiness in any way they could. Most of the time we fought over my mother. I was either sticking up for her or defending my ability to step outside her shadow and learn from her mistakes. I had been told nothing but horrible things about my grandparents for as long as I could remember. She never said anything good about them. This caused me to behave rather foolishly throughout my adolescence. For instance, one time, my grandfather and I got into a fight over something and he raised his hand to me. I got up in his face and asked him to hit me, but he just poked me in the chest until I backed down. They were so terrified that I would turn out like her that they wouldn't let me do anything she had done at my age. I spent many of my teenage years apologizing for my misconceptions and I hold a great deal of remorse for the way I treated them growing up. They were only doing their best and I was not very cooperative. I pretended that everything in my life was fine, but on the inside I was struggling.

Then came Amanda's surprise birthday party. My friend Sydney and I had it all planned out, right down to the cake! We invited all of our close friends. At that time we were still hanging out with the same group from our eighth grade class. There was Chris, whom I dated for a short time after our D.C. trip. We never officially broke up, but with everything that happened with my mother that summer, we basically just drifted apart. There were no hard feelings, in fact it eventually just became a joke between us. Chris was hilarious; a true comedian. He had a heavy build, long hair, and he exuded *grunge*. He could entertain for hours and was the life of the party on many occasions. Randy was a tall ginger with a love for the theater. He and Chris were in several of our high school plays that year together and they were great. I always expected to see them on the big screen someday and hopefully I will. I met Sydney in fifth grade. She is truly one of the nicest people you will ever meet. She had beautiful long brown hair that she usually kept pulled back and captivatingly blue eyes. Tim was a bit of an odd duck, but we all embraced his crazy antics. He was about the size of a toothpick, with jet black hair that he combed over to one side of his head like a balding man would do. He had a huge crush on Amanda, so it was not surprising when he suggested we have the party at his place.

Tim's parents said we could have it in their basement, and Chris and Randy said they would help decorate. Sydney and I got balloons and made a really fun cake that I found the recipe for in one of my grandmother's magazines. We used a bundt cake pan and covered the cake in blue frosting. Grandma found me a margarita umbrella and I used a piece of cinnamon gum for a diving board. We used colored frosting to draw bathing suits and swim trunks on teddy-bear-shaped graham crackers, and then placed them around the ocean-colored frosting for the full effect. It was just before Christmas, so the theme didn't really fit, but we didn't care. It was clever-looking and super easy to make! Everyone rendezvoused at Tim's house and waited while Tim's dad and I went to pick up Amanda and take her to dinner, although I told her it was my uncle who was taking us and we blindfolded her so she would be surprised. As we pulled into Tim's driveway, the feeling of anticipation was palpable. I helped her out of the car and around the back of the house. I could tell she thought something was off, but the surprise was so close it didn't matter. Chris opened the door and I lead Amanda in and seated her at the "table." Then, just as the incense began to alert her to the fact that she wasn't in a restaurant, we took off the blindfold and everyone screamed: Surprise! Happiness ensued and all was wonderful. We laughed and laughed; it was so fun!

In the days that followed, perhaps one of the most challenging events was Christmas. It was the first Christmas after Mom had left. Having my mother around for the past few years on Christmas made getting ready for this one somewhat difficult. The day after Thanksgiving was when we usually filled the house with Christmas music and spent the whole day putting up lights and decorations. Then after dinner we'd put up and decorate the tree. We always used the same fake tree instead of cutting down a living one; my mother always thought that was mean. That year I vowed to carry on the tradition, regardless of whether she came home or not, so I did. My grandparents humored my obnoxious caroling and commented from time to time on how nice all the decorations looked. I worked all day and after it was finished and I turned on the lights, a sense of empowerment flowed through my veins! It may seem a small event to some, but at that very moment, I knew I was going to be okay. I had proven to myself that I didn't need her to carry on tradition; I could do it on my own! A part of me was terrified of my mom and of what she was capable. The question always lingered: Even if she does come home, will she stay? After that day, it didn't matter, because when and if she does, I know I'll always be okay!

Afterword

My mother remained missing for the duration of my high school years. At a time when I needed her most. Milestone after milestone without her to share them with. There were homecoming dances, boyfriends, sporting competitions, and all of the usual coming-of-age moments one would expect in a young teenage girl's life.

Perhaps the most disheartening of these were prom and graduation. In the back of my mind, I always thought that she would make it back to us by the time these events took place. When prom came and went, I still held on to the hope that she would somehow make it to my graduation. I would fantasize about her showing up to surprise me on that day. I envisioned stepping into the crowd of family and friends to find her waiting for me in the shadows.

I knew that meant she would have been arrested directly after our embrace, but it would be as if she chose to sacrifice her freedom to see her one and only daughter graduate high school. Much to my disappointment, this did not happen. However, shortly after graduation, my mother was found and she continues to keep me on my toes. I thought my childhood was interesting, but I had no idea what was in store for me in the years to come!

About the Author

Tiffany Rochelle is an artist and freelance writer who holds a degree in psychology from the University of Washington. She lives in Denver, Colorado